LIFE NATURE LIBRARY

THE LAND AND WILDLIFE OF

TROPICAL
ASIA

OTHER BOOKS
BY THE EDITORS OF LIFE

LIFE NATURE LIBRARY

THE LAND AND WILDLIFE OF
TROPICAL ASIA

by S. Dillon Ripley
and The Editors of LIFE

TIME INCORPORATED

NEW YORK

A
STONEHENGE
BOOK

About the Author

Sidney Dillon Ripley describes himself as an "old-fashioned naturalist of the Darwin school . . . interested in everything in nature." Unlike Darwin, who went on his first expedition at the ripe old age of 22, Ripley was only 13 when he and his 20-year-old sister hiked through western Tibet studying birds. After graduating from Yale in 1936 he decided to "abandon all thoughts of a prosperous and worthy future" and as a migrant ornithologist embarked for India, Nepal and points east, where he became fluent in several tropical Asian languages. He returned to the U.S. in 1940 and received his Ph.D. in zoology from Harvard in 1943. The war intervened and he was appointed chief of OSS Intelligence in Ceylon, where he supervised a secret agent training program. He has returned to tropical Asia several times since the war and has written five books on ornithological subjects, including *A Paddling of Ducks*, *Search for the Spiny Babbler* and *Trail of the Money Bird*. Since World War II he has been on the biology faculty at Yale and in 1959 he became director of Yale's Peabody Museum of Natural History, a position he held until 1964, when he was appointed Secretary of The Smithsonian Institution. Mr. Ripley is married and has three daughters.

ON THE COVER: An Indian rhinoceros, its mudbath reverie disrupted, retreats into the elephant grass. The mistaken notion that rhino horn is an aphrodisiac was one factor that led this once-numerous species to the brink of extinction.

Contents

TIME-LIFE BOOKS

EDITOR
Norman P. Ross
TEXT DIRECTOR   **ART DIRECTOR**
William Jay Gold   Edward A. Hamilton
CHIEF OF RESEARCH
Beatrice T. Dobie
Assistant Text Director: Jerry Korn
Assistant Chief of Research: Monica O. Horne

•

PUBLISHER
Rhett Austell
General Manager: John A. Watters
Business Manager: John D. McSweeney
Circulation Manager: Joan D. Lanning

LIFE MAGAZINE

EDITOR: Edward K. Thompson
MANAGING EDITOR: George P. Hunt
PUBLISHER: Jerome S. Hardy

LIFE NATURE LIBRARY

EDITOR: Maitland A. Edey
Associate Editor: Percy Knauth
Assistants to the Editor: Robert Morton, John Porter
Designer: Paul Jensen
Staff Writers: Dale Brown, Timothy Carr,
Mary Louise Grossman, Peter Wood
Chief Researcher: Martha Turner
Researchers: Jane Alexander, David Bridge, Doris Bry,
Peggy Bushong, Joan Chasin, Nancy Jacobsen,
Paula Norworth, Carol Phillippe, Marjorie Pickens,
Susan Rayfield, Carollee Rosenblatt, Roxanna Sayre,
Nancy Shuker, Iris Unger, John von Hartz

EDITORIAL PRODUCTION
Art Associate: Robert L. Young
Art Assistants: James D. Smith, Mark A. Binn, John Newcomb
Picture Researchers: Margaret K. Goldsmith, Barbara Sullivan
Copy Staff: Marian Gordon Goldman, Joan Chambers,
Dolores A. Littles

The text for this book is by S. Dillon Ripley, the picture essays by the editorial staff. The following individuals and departments of Time Inc. helped to produce the book: Margaret Bourke-White, James Burke, John Dominis, Eliot Elisofon, Dmitri Kessel, Nina Leen and Michael Rougier, LIFE staff photographers; Doris O'Neil, Chief, LIFE Picture Library; Richard M. Clurman, Chief, TIME-LIFE News Service; and Content Peckham, Chief, Bureau of Editorial Reference.

Introduction

IT is perhaps a little out of fashion, in these cosmo-astronautic times, to come down to earth flatly and boast on a mere subcontinental scale. But right here let it be declared that Southeast Asia has, on any countdown, as varied and exotic plants, as wide (and wild) an assemblage of animals as can be found anywhere in this known world. Up until now, no one book has successfully painted across this vivid canvas. It has not been possible—either for the naturalist or plain looker-on—to get a proper view. The natural history of other continents is becoming well known, but this huge slice of Asia has remained an area of remarkable biological ignorance and frequently actual misinformation.

This ignorance is not confined to persons *outside* Southeast Asia. Those who live here—as I have for 19 years—find it tremendously difficult to see the woods for the giant trees; to achieve any kind of familiarity with a forest that is drenched by 100 or more inches of rain a year; to get to know animals that are active only at night—as are tarsier and loris, frog and frogmouth, civet, civet cat and flying lemur. This book, therefore, pioneers to a double purpose. It tells the Westerner about nature in Southeast Asia. It tells Southeast Asia about its own somewhat underestimated natural self. It is compulsory reading in Borneo as much as in Brooklyn, along the Irrawaddy as much as beside the Thames.

The author, S. Dillon Ripley, is a distinguished ornithologist and is one of the few long-time, deep and intimate experts and lovers of Asian wildlife. It is appropriate that while actually writing this book, he was appointed to the top post in the world of international natural history: Secretary of the Smithsonian Institution in Washington, D.C. Yet he maintains close field contacts with those of us who stay and sweat it out down in the region—as even we in this small, remote land know from his continued encouragement and personal generosity. Probably only LIFE and he could have gathered, inside one cover, the many facts and the beautiful and informative pictures that this book contains.

TOM HARRISSON
Director, Sarawak Museum
Kuching, Malaysia

LIKE PANES OF GLASS, PADDIES IN THAILAND SHIMMER IN THE SUN. BEHIND THEM FLOWS THE MEKONG, CALLED A SECOND NILE BECAUSE ITS

1 The Southeastern Realm

FLOODS BRING RICH SILT TO THE LOWLANDS. SOUTHEAST ASIA'S LONGEST RIVER, IT RISES IN TIBET AND EMPTIES INTO THE SEA, 2,600 MILES AWAY

I N all the grand design of nature no area of the world is more richly endowed
with forms of life than tropical Asia and its widely scattered archipelagoes of
neighbor islands. Here, from the plains of India eastward through the Indochinese peninsula and along all the outflung fingers of the Malay arc, is a land
unique and munificent in its proliferation of species. Alfred Russel Wallace,
the great naturalist who coincidentally with Charles Darwin put forth the theory of evolution by natural selection, found his chief source of inspiration here
and was moved to describe the wealth of the islands in memorable words:

THE LAND TAKES SHAPE

The five maps on these pages trace in rough outline the geological development of tropical Asia from the start of the Cenozoic, some 63 million years ago, to the present. In contrast to the rest of Asia, this area seems always to have been one of great instability, subject to periodic mountain building and volcanic activity, inundations by the sea, the making and unmaking of islands, and the formation and disintegration of land bridges. Girdled by volcanoes, the island festoons of tropical Asia continue to be affected by geological unrest: Indonesia has, on the average, an earthquake a day.

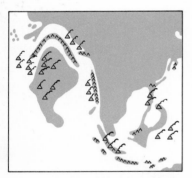

PALEOCENE

Tropical Asia began to take on a recognizable shape some 63 million years ago, during a period of volcanic activity and mountain building. India at this time was an island; part of Burma a seagirt mountain chain with offshore volcanoes.

EOCENE

Ten million years later the furious volcanic and mountain activity had nearly ceased on the mainland but it still continued in Indonesia. This was a period of great geological calm, with a high sea level that drowned many small islands.

"Bathed by the tepid water of the great tropical oceans, this region enjoys a climate more uniformly hot and moist than almost any other part of the globe, and teems with natural productions which are elsewhere unknown. The richest of fruits and the most precious of species are here indigenous. It produces the giant flowers of the Rafflesia, the great green-winged Ornithoptera (princes among the butterfly tribes), the man-like Orang-Utan, and the gorgeous birds of Paradise." And nothing has occurred in the century or so since Wallace thus described it to change the fascination of the area. Although tens of thousands of species have been described here, more remain unknown, more still await discovery, than in any other region of the earth.

GEOGRAPHICALLY, the region of tropical Asia does not loom significantly on the globe. Many maps show the islands of which it is largely composed scaled so as to appear small. It is hard to realize that, for example, the Malay Archipelago stretches for nearly 4,000 miles from west to east. These are dimensions on a continental order, yet the Oriental region, the zoogeographical name chosen by Wallace for the area, as a whole is larger still. Essentially it consists of the peninsula of India, reaching north to the foothills of the Himalayas and south to include Ceylon, and then sweeping east through Pakistan, the Andaman and Nicobar Islands to Burma, Thailand and the Indochinese peninsula to southeastern China, including the island of Hainan. Farther south still are the islands of the Indonesian arc east to the Lesser Sundas, the Moluccas and finally the Philippines.

This is an imposing area indeed, and a formidable one to get to know on the ground. Nor is it any easier by water. In its westernmost part, there is a certain simplicity about the great plains and rolling hills which start below the Himalayas, fanning south and east; but soon, as one goes east and south, the fierce running of rivers and great mountain ranges coming down and crisscrossing the pattern of the land make any journey difficult. The overland traveler, for instance, who succeeds in reaching Singapore from India by car still rates a hero's welcome at the Raffles Hotel—and once past Singapore, there are more than 3,000 miles, west to east, crowded with thousands of islands of every shape and size, including the third and fourth largest of the world. The seas are technically charted but to navigate all of them would take a lifetime. The Bugis, the classical sailors of Southeast Asia, regularly take three months or more to sail from Celebes around the huge bulge of Borneo, south, west and then northwest, up into the entrepôt of Singapore.

Only in a balloon, drifting, could man perhaps capture in a single journey the real feel of Southeast Asia. There does not happen to be a northwesterly prevailing wind fanning across this region, but if there were one, the slow and leisurely pace of a balloon wafted along by it would be ideal—far better suited for a survey of the land than the sonic speed of modern jet travel. And once the savannas and plains of northwest India were crossed, two impressions would be dominant: first, the extent to which, in many areas, man's two principal crops of rice and rubber have replaced the original vegetation; and second, the far more impressive extent to which original vegetation—i.e., rain forest—still prevails. There would be hundreds of miles over the Malay Peninsula, for instance, in which the landscape below was a solid carpet of rubber trees, days of ballooning across Indochina in which it was a patchwork of rice paddies—but there could be further hundreds of miles in which billions of jungle trees succeeded each other in unbroken ranks along every ridge right out to the horizon, a canopy of evergreen wilderness shielding a hidden world all its own.

Such are the powerful contrasts of the Southeast Asian region. Where man has subdued and destroyed the jungle, well over 95 per cent of the kinds of living things, plant and animal, have no place; yet even there will be found beauties and curiosities—fine butterflies, strange lizards, noisy bulbuls, unlimited ants. Nowhere in Southeast Asia is life weak or meager, even where man has laid his heaviest hand. Where he has not, it burgeons in unrivaled variety and splendor.

This is a tropical region which combines elements of a very ancient world with elements of a world still in the active stages of building. Whereas on the west the Oriental region rests on an old and permanent continental foundation in India, much of its southeastern part is an area of great instability, with eruptive volcanoes and islands still rising out of the sea. But one of the most important geological features can be distinguished in the wide, shallow seas stretching between the arcs of the East Indian archipelago and the southeast coast of the Asian continent. The seas here cover a great shelf which is now known to have been only recently submerged at the end of the Pleistocene.

This shelf, known as the Sunda Shelf, represents one of the three great natural divisions in this part of the world. Another, the Sahul Shelf, comprises the submerged northern extension of Australia. Between the two shelves lies the third division, the twisted chains of the East Indian archipelago, including the Lesser Sunda Islands, Celebes and the Moluccas, where volcanoes flare and boom, where some of the islands are still rising at a slow but measurable rate, where high mountain peaks plunge steeply to depths of 30,000 feet below the sea. This is a typical "arc of instability," where the earth's crust is still under tremendous pressure, buckling and folding. Here, even today, we can glimpse the major drama of Southeast Asia's geological evolution, for volcanoes and the instability they represent played an important part in the history of the area.

THE close relationship between the Asian continent and the islands is distinctly seen in the mountains of the area. As a matter of fact, the islands may be said to be welded to the continent by an active process of mountain building. Positioned in linear fashion throughout the larger islands, as well as in the Lesser Sunda Islands, the mountains arc up through the Malay Peninsula and Burma to the Himalayan system, where they are connected northeast of India in Assam. They form one of the greatest mountain belts of the world, comparable in length to that of the Andes in South America, and are not only one of the most remarkable topographical features of Southeast Asia but have had an effect of marked importance on its climate and on the distribution and evolution of the fauna and flora.

Although great changes occurred throughout geological time, it was really within the Pleistocene, the last million or so years of the earth's history, that the most important events shaping the distribution, in particular of vertebrates of the Oriental region, took place. These were the ice ages, four major cycles of alternating cold and warm climates in the more northern latitudes, during the colder phases of which the level of the seas dropped so far that connections emerged between the islands of the Sunda Shelf. These falls and rises of the sea at various times connected much of the Malay Archipelago with the mainland, then broke the connections into thousands of islands once again.

This erratic sequence of continuity and discontinuity has complicated the sequence and movement of all sorts of animals into and through the southern

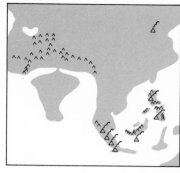

MIOCENE

By 25 million years ago, mountain building had resumed, and the first main upthrust of what was to be the Himalayas appeared. This rising of the land narrowed the sea arms that previously separated India from the main continent.

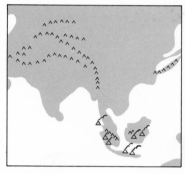

PLIOCENE

About 13 million years ago the joining of India and mainland was completed. The Himalayas continued to grow. In the southeast, eruptions continued to plague the unstable islands; rising seas narrowed the future Malay Peninsula.

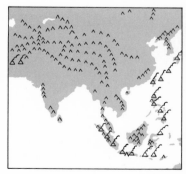

PRESENT

The Himalayas today, still rising, are part of the largest mountain chain in the world. Volcanic activity has peppered the waters of Southeast Asia with innumerable islands and archipelagoes, many of them born during the last million years.

part of the area. Most of these ups and downs, furthermore, occurred after the evolution of the higher mammals, but they still affected the evolution of many of the species, including the higher primates like the orangutan and man. This has had a particular bearing on the distribution and gathering strength of human types, and on how, in the end, they came to dominate the entire natural history of Southeast Asia—a matter with which we shall deal extensively in a later chapter of this book.

But as well as the successive lowerings and risings of the seas in the area of the Malay Archipelago, there is another factor of importance which has accompanied the distribution and development of its flora and fauna—the activities of volcanoes. While it has been known for some time that volcanoes have been prominent here, the most recent research, conducted with the latest methods of dating, has now shown that volcanic activity took place in areas where it had previously been unsuspected. For example, not long ago geological explorations in central Borneo yielded evidence that at least several hundred square miles of the remote interior, now covered by rain forest and completely virgin wilderness, was subject to major volcanic activity in the latter part of the Pleistocene, perhaps as little as 50,000 years ago. This is only one of several indications which encourage scientists to consider that relatively large land alterations due to volcanic eruptions have been more widespread than previously thought, and that they have occurred since as well as before the time span of Java man and Peking man, some 360,000 years ago.

The continuation of geological instability right up to the present day is of the greatest importance in interpreting the present picture of animal and plant life in this area. For instance, in the center of some of the islands, there are extensive areas where the rain forest seems to have been set on fire a very long time ago, on such a scale that the original vegetation has never been replaced and a peculiar sort of poor secondary jungle has developed instead. This, too, has not yet been satisfactorily explained. It would be impossible for early man to fire such great tracts of humid, tropical rain forest, but it can be presumed that the firing was done by volcanic means.

It is interesting to note that this whole matter of Southeast Asia's explosively volcanic past is reflected in other ways than just in rocks and mountains—it is, in fact, reflected in the conscious and subconscious memories of man. Most of the people of Southeast Asia were until recently almost wholly illiterate. Countless tribes, like the Karens of Burma, the Bataks of Sumatra, the Dayaks of Borneo, could preserve a record of the past only in sagas and folk songs, and they have done so, in enormous volume and vivid detail. Memorized and passed on through countless generations, these tales are full of dramatic events which, even in widely separated places, have a certain basic similarity: they tell, among other things, of struggles with volcanic powers, of a great fire mountain which is eventually quelled by a kindlier mountain of water or solid earth.

Thus, far back into the half-world of primitive memory, the deep feeling of this Asian folklore reflects the geological unrest of the area. And as a result, the sense of nature in the people is not, as might be expected in an environment so exceptionally equable in climate, in any way static or secure. They seed their rice and harvest it year after year with seemingly unshakable regularity, yet each year the harvest comes anew as a sensational surprise. Is this not characteristic of people whose very belief in the idea of a universe stems from an explosive past?

The great forests and jungles of the Oriental region, its dominant glory, have been known for centuries to the Western world, from Ptolemy's Second Century geography through Marco Polo and subsequent travelers to the dazzling accounts of 18th and 19th Century explorers and naturalists. Long before, however, Asians had penetrated into the secrets of the continent's southeast and the remoter islands. Indian sailors traded there as early as the Sixth Century B.C., while Chinese of the Han empire had trading stations along the coasts of the islands and even penetrated into the wild hinterland of Borneo at least 700 years before the first Europeans. They traded for rhinoceros horns, hornbill ivory, edible bird's nests, dammar gum, wild rubber and rattan vines, bringing glass beads and stoneware jars which remain to this day the most valued treasures of the remotest tribes. By the Third and Fourth Centuries A.D. the Persian traders were well entrenched in this area and their ships were commonplace as far as the ports of China. Eight hundred years before Europeans realized that the earth was round, Persian, Indian and Malay ships carried T'ang pottery, bronze and silk from China to the islands, ending there a Stone Age which farther east, in central New Guinea, has persisted into the 20th Century. In the 12th Century, under the Sung Dynasty, China itself became a great sea power, advanced in ship building and design as well as in the science of navigation, and it carried its own products to the great seaports of the islands, the Strait of Malacca and farther north along the coasts of the Malay Peninsula. The scale of all this trade was enormous, as recent excavations have shown. In site after site—sometimes in places now entirely overrun by mangrove swamp and changes in estuary formation—the broken shards of discarded pottery and glass can be taken out by the truckload.

THE bulk of this trade was for spices, valuable woods, even gold and tin— but the Chinese, then as now, also had strange ideas about the physical or medical effects of animal products which were unfamiliar to them at home. The native peoples with whom they dealt evidently fostered this mystery. Very wisely they did not let the traders know the truth about some of the things they were prepared to barter for so highly. So it is difficult to sort out, from the early T'ang and Sung Chinese records, exactly what the treasurers and accountants of those days thought they were recording. Edible bird's nests got mixed up with edible fungus, which they do curiously resemble to the prescientific eye. Beeswax and honey got confused with what the early Chinese annals called "stone honey"; stone honey got mixed up with actual stalactites and stalagmites which were broken off and traded by the Bataks, Malays and Dayaks. One specialty which greatly attracted the Chinese was the internal casts of the beautifully shaped shells proliferating on the limestone hills of the islands, where almost every hill offered its own special shape, often exquisite. Under suitable conditions, after a few centuries in a cave or flood bed of a side stream, the limestone filled the shell, while the shell itself dissolved to leave a delicate, strangely shaped object, solid and puzzling to the uninitiated. Far back, these shell casts were dug out and sold to the Chinese in exchange for the sorts of pots and bowls which any Western museum would now be glad to pay handsomely for in its Oriental collections. Also traded in this way were the small blue plumes of the white-collared kingfisher, used in the headdresses of actors and courtesans; the scales of the pangolin, or scaly anteater, a mystical cure for ringworm; and deer antlers, which were ground up as a fever cure.

Unfortunately for our record here, this pattern of misinformation—or perhaps

A GIANT COMES TO BLOOM

Rafflesia, the world's largest flower, first appears as a bulge in the cracked bark of a ground-trailing liana (top). Drawing nourishment from the sap of the vine, it slowly grows bigger until, after about nine months, it is the size of a man's head (center). Cabbagelike in appearance, the mature bud contains the sexual apparatus of the flower, here that of a female (bottom). The speckled part is the ovary; the cones are sterile protuberances; the area between cones and ovary secretes the flower's characteristic foul odor. Unfolded, the bloom can be a yard across and, after being fertilized by insects, it rots to a soggy mass on the forest floor. Its sticky seeds are believed to be distributed by animals that either eat them or brush against them and later drop them, sometimes on the bark or exposed roots of other lianas.

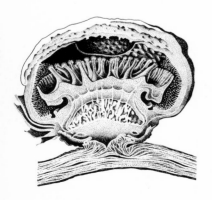

it was simply good business discretion—has meant that little in the Chinese and other early records can be relied upon as descriptive and truthful for natural history. A rhinoceros easily became a unicorn and was so described by Marco Polo. The huge helmeted hornbill, which produced a raw material more esteemed than jade for mandarins' elaborately carved belt buckles, was happily transformed into a phoenix. Nor did the first white traders from the west do much better in this field. Like Marco Polo, they had disappointingly little to say on anything of animals or plants—these earliest outsiders were dazzled by the abundance and vitality of Asian human life and riches, but they scarcely saw the trees for the palaces, the birds for the pearls and embroidery. The Portuguese, who first really settled down to study Southeast Asia from 1511 on, spent most of their time trying to get rich. At that time this was not easy. In effect they were largely preoccupied with fighting and killing—and being killed if not massacred by pirates and local tribes. As the people got more used to such interventions, chances for friendliness grew, and with these the opportunities for white men to travel more widely on land and learn a little more of nature's richness there.

The true, classic, virgin rain forest remains in pure and massive extent mostly along the northern fringes of the island area, down the central span of the Malay Archipelago, and in the central uplands of the heart of Borneo and Sumatra. It is salutary to remember that recently a naturalist traveled with experience and speed for 26 days through one part of central Borneo without coming out into open sunlight or any place of past or present cultivation. But with the population explosion and economic expansion of every nation in Southeast Asia, such lonely achievements may well be inconceivable by the end of this century.

As we examine the basic structure and essential history of this tropical region, we must always bear clearly in mind that a great deal of what we shall hereafter write about and illustrate belongs to the life of the rain forest. This is a difficult place, and to the inexperienced it can be very depressing. The utmost skill is needed to move about without treading on twigs or disturbing some creature which will trigger a warning for minutes and miles ahead, alerting every monkey and woodpecker that his least-favorite animal, man, is approaching. To stand stock-still is the best way to observe; it is also the best way of attracting a wonderful variety of biting insects, of which each country and every district in Southeast Asia have some specialty—the sand fly, the deer fly, the sweat bee, more than 30 species of mosquitoes, the hornet or what have you. Once patience has been acquired, the rewards are enormous. Even so, no one observer can hope to see more than a fraction of the whole pattern in this tropical cornucopia. On the other hand, with luck he is quite likely to see new things, even new species not known before to any man.

We shall have much more to say about the rain forest later on. For the moment, let us consider as examples of its diverse plant and animal life three of the species which attracted Wallace's attention: the giant flower *Rafflesia*, the great, green-winged butterfly *Ornithoptera*, and the manlike ape, the orangutan.

Rafflesia, discovered by and named for that omnivorous naturalist-collector Sir Thomas Stamford Raffles, is the largest land-growing flower anywhere. The Sumatran species, *Rafflesia arnoldi*, has blooms more than three feet across, the huge petals a brilliant scarlet dotted with white, spreading outward from an extraordinary white bowl which could easily hold a couple of gallons of water. No less extraordinary than its vivid color and size is its powerful and putrid smell, an odor of extraordinary intensity which has the function of attracting flies and other insects that infest the flowers in great numbers.

Adding to their astonishing character is the fact that these enormous flowers appear erratically and in rare places on the jungle floor. A *Rafflesia* plant first shows as a bud, which develops into what looks like a big brown cabbage. The bud, growing from funguslike tissues which parasitize the underground roots of trees, may take as much as nine months to mature. Then suddenly it explodes into its sensational blossom, usually only one flower at one place at one time, with no other surrounding blooms or leaves.

Rafflesia fascinated Wallace, and it has fascinated others since his time, yet it is characteristic that there are botanists who have spent years in Southeast Asia without ever finding a single bloom.

Just as strange and beautiful in its way is Wallace's *Ornithoptera*, which he called "princes among butterfly tribes." *Ornithoptera* means "birdwing," and he gave the name to "one of the most elegant species known," *Ornithoptera brookeana*, discovered in Borneo and named for the first white rajah, Sir James Brooke. Although entomologists of Brazil, pointing to the wealth of species in that land, disagree, most others consider Brooke's birdwing the most tastefully elegant and colorfully perfect of its kind. Velvet black, it is dressed with a curved band of vivid metallic-green spots across the wings from tip to tip, each spot shaped like a tiny feather, and a broad crimson collar.

Wallace thought the birdwing rare, but it has since been found all over the area with a number of racial varieties. It is often seen in company with other butterflies, sipping with long proboscis at spring seepages, riverbanks, on spongy mosses, among sunny rocks or even, if near human habitation, on urine and the damp droppings of cattle. But those which are readily seen are nearly all male; the female *Ornithoptera brookeana* is still rare. Even Wallace never found one. The sex ratio was long believed to run into hundreds and in some places thousands to one in favor of the beautiful male, but this is probably not the case. The female, larger and duller, remains a rarity in collections primarily because she hardly ever leaves the high canopy of the trees and so can seldom be observed.

Third, Wallace starred the orangutan. Indeed, to study this great ape was one of the primary reasons why he chose to go to Southeast Asia. He gives it special mention in the subtitle of his book, *The Malay Archipelago*, and the frontispiece shows an enormous orangutan biting a large chunk out of a nearly naked Dayak. The picture is highly misleading. The orangutan, not quite as large as the gorilla, not quite as superficially smart as the chimpanzee, is actually the gentlest, most sensitive and most independent of the great apes. It never attacks man unless infuriated by him. Wallace was fascinated by orangs and even adopted an orphaned orang infant which had yet to cut its first teeth and which he cared for with extraordinary tenderness. To keep his little Mias— as the natives called the orang—warm and comfortable the busy naturalist fitted out a small box for a cradle, with a small mat for the baby to lie on which was changed and washed every day. He bathed his little pet regularly and noted that it "enjoyed the wiping and rubbing dry amazingly, and when I brushed its hair it seemed to be perfectly happy, lying quite still with its arms and legs stretched out while I thoroughly brushed the long hair of its back and arms." He made a ladder for it to hang on and also an artificial mother, wrapping a piece of buffalo skin into a bundle which he suspended about a foot from the floor within the infant's reach. At first this proved quite successful, and the baby orang was obviously pleased—until it attempted to get milk from the substitute parent. Since all it could get for its efforts to suck was a mouthful of wool and hair on which it almost choked to death, Wallace was obliged to take the imitation mother away again.

When Wallace came into the Oriental region the orangutan population numbered several millions and centered in Borneo and part of Sumatra. Its placid temperament and almost scientific curiosity led this great ape to be fearless of and even positively interested in its cousin, man. Yet orangs already had become extinct in Celebes and Java, possibly exterminated by superstitious human populations way back in the Stone Age. The evidence is in abundant remains found by Dutch archeologists in limestone caves.

Wallace, a naturalist in the mood of his time, initiated a new and more efficient slaughter with the modern technology of the rifle. He was interested in collecting specimens, and he describes in horrible detail how he virtually massacred orangs as they looked down at him from the treetops. Early men may have killed orangutans from superstitious fear; now the whole idea of evolutionary theory suddenly put a premium on ape-man ideas. Everybody wanted to prove or disprove something about our supposed near-ancestors, and specimens for dissection were in enormous demand. The literature of Southeast Asia for the next 50 years contains a chronicle of orang slaughter amounting to something like genocide. The American naturalist William Hornaday collected over 50; he was subsequently to turn against the principle of wholesale collecting and become a noted conservationist who played a vital role in saving the American buffalo and helped to found the New York Zoological Society. But as late as 1894 a Swiss who went hunting orangs for a collector in Basel shot and sent back to Europe 134 specimens. Orangs could still be shot all over the place, and easily.

Today, it is a different story. In 1963, a Japanese zoologist, Dr. K. Yoshiba of the Japanese Monkey Center, spent three months out in the best orang jungle remaining in Borneo and never succeeded in seeing one. Barbara Harrisson, wife of the curator of the Sarawak Museum, who has spent several years studying orangs, reckons that under ideal conditions three hours visual contact a week is a real attainment. In fact, the orang is now rare, shy and faced with extinction. It is not used as food; the decline to a few hundred survivors is largely the result of collecting for museums and latterly zoos. And, sadly enough, we still know practically nothing about the natural life, social organization and habits of this ape.

These three illustrations from Wallace—the giant plant, the glorious butterfly and the vanishing ape—indicate two things vital from the beginning for an understanding of the natural history of the tropical Asian region: first, the breadth, the range and strangeness of its life; second, that although so much has been studied and collected and written, so much remains unknown, even about the most striking and attractive of the region's living creatures.

To bring into focus and make intelligible this teeming life therefore presents some special difficulties—not encountered at all, for instance, if we were writing about North America, Europe or the Antarctic. But though this may be a disadvantage in obtaining simplicity, the variety of interest is so great that we can dip anywhere in the region, into any branch of the animal or plant kingdom, and at once find something fascinating in itself.

THE DRY EARTH OF NORTHWESTERN INDIA GIVES NO HINT THAT TO THE SOUTHEAST THE LANDS OF TROPICAL ASIA ARE MOIST AND GREEN

A Land of Water and Fire

The forces of geological change seem accelerated in tropical Asia. Here, rain is more than rain—it is an erosive torrent that loosens soil from the mountainsides and feeds it to swollen rivers. Floods dump silt on fertile deltas, continually building them out into shallow seas, and on the islands, volcanoes bury old contours under layers of ash while streams of lava create new land forms.

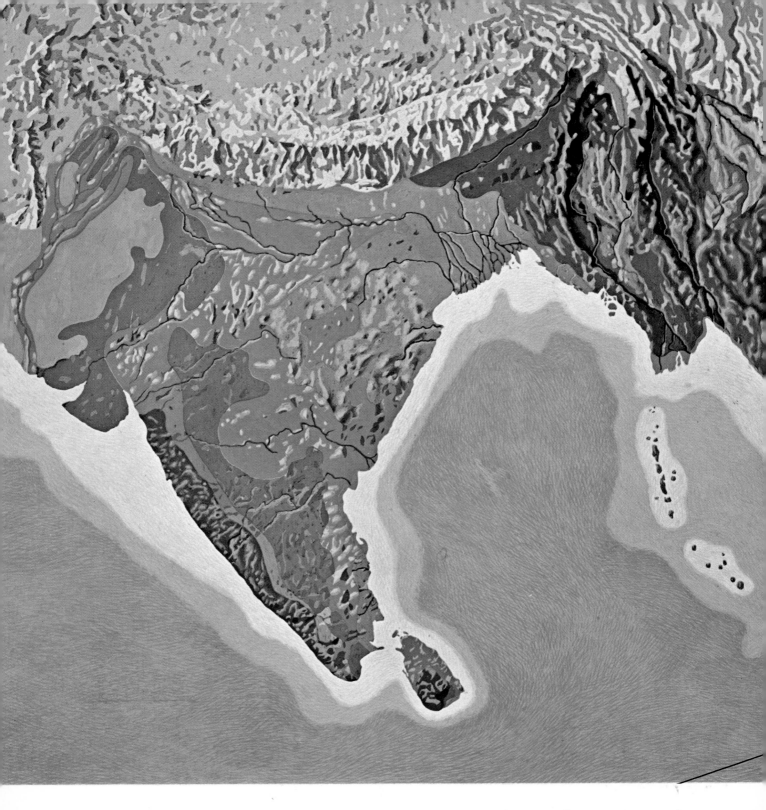

THE VEGETATION OF

TROPICAL
ASIA

Rain and heat work together to make tropical Asia one of the world's most richly vegetated areas. Where the rainfall is heaviest, as in the islands and along the Malay Peninsula, rain forest prevails, but where a wet season is followed by a rainless one, as in northern parts of the region, a monsoon forest dominates the land. This is a peculiar forest: leafless and barren during the dry months, it springs to life with the coming of the rains, bursting into bloom and growing lush and thick. Heavy rains have also helped to produce the

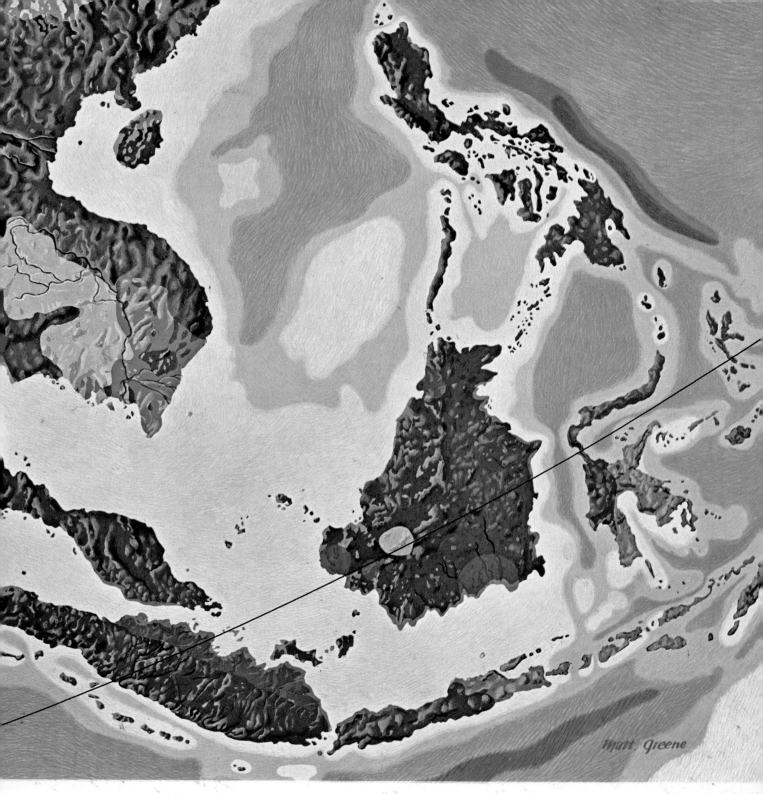

mangrove swamps and marshy peat forests along the coasts. The mangrove swamps give some idea of the volume of silt brought down from the land by the rivers and, together with debris washed in from the sea, held in place by the spidery roots of the trees. The peat forests, in turn, reflect the volume of water falling on the land: the soil here is so waterlogged bacteria cannot convert fallen vegetable matter into humus. Such damp areas contrast markedly with the drier parts of western India, where desert scrub and thorn forest dominate.

 TROPICAL RAIN FOREST

 MONSOON FOREST

 THORN FOREST

 DRY TROPICAL (DECIDUOUS)

 SWAMP PEAT FOREST

 SAVANNA

 MANGROVE SWAMP

 DESERT SCRUB

The Disappearing Mountains

Without precipices, with no sharp peaks, these rolling slopes on Ceylon suggest hills rather than mountains. Yet mountains they are, ranging up to 8,292 feet, though like so many others throughout tropical Asia they give little hint that once they stood more than half as high as the Himalayas, the great, jagged range which forms the region's northern border. Today the mountains of tropical Asia have been cut down to size by eons of erosive rains. Only the active volcanoes show a barren wildness, and even they shrink drastically with a dimming of their fires. All but the

Central highlands near Kandy, Ceylon

highest peaks have been tamed in another way as well—by the vegetation that covers them. Because of the warm, damp climate, plants grow much farther up the slopes and in much greater profusion than in such temperate zone ranges as the Rockies or Alps, and their dense, green canopy and mat of humus conceal the rock core. In this area a phenomenon called "creep" is prevalent: on steep hillsides gravity pulls whole slopes, plants and all, with glacial slowness down over the wet bedrock—a movement which, when the rains come, may turn into a full-fledged avalanche.

21

The Beneficent Rivers

Born in mountains and highlands near the heart of the continent, the major rivers of tropical Asia—the Brahmaputra, the Ganges, the Irrawaddy, the Salween and the Mekong *(right)*—exert tremendous influence over the land. Swollen with seasonal rains, dyed with mud and sand washed down from the hills, they may rise as much as 90 feet, bulldoze out their channels and sweep over their banks across flood plains many miles wide. In their roiled waters, they carry rich silt downstream, pouring it onto fields or building it up into deltas where it can eventually be put to agricultural use. The volume of silt is enormous. India's Ganges and Brahmaputra, combining into a single stream at Goalundo, have laid down a 20,000-square-mile delta, the world's largest. In one day the streams on the island of Java strip their drainage basins of as much earth as France's Marne does in two centuries, and the Irrawaddy in Burma contains about one and a half pounds of silt per cubic yard, as compared to two ounces for the Seine or Rhine.

22

Mekong River at Luang Prabang, Laos

Tree ferns in Malaya

The Indispensable Forests

Were it not for thick forests which hold the soil on mountain slopes and lowland, the torrential rains of tropical Asia would long ago have swept most of the earth away. But often the trees exist in precarious balance with the environment. In the hotter, damper parts of the region, bacteria break down dead vegetable matter almost faster than it can be replaced, and the warm, heavy rains that dissolve the more soluble compounds also leach these from the soil before they can be fully utilized by plants as food. Thus where a forest has been cut and the delicate balance upset, trees may be long returning. And the soil, now low in organic content, tends to redden with the chemically more resistant iron and aluminum compounds and harden upon exposure to air; sometimes it solidifies into the durable stone with which temples of Angkor *(opposite)* were built nearly 1,000 years ago.

Temple of Prah Kahn, Cambodia

25

The Renewing Volcanoes

Volcanoes play a major role in the life of much of tropical Asia. The Philippines, where this photograph was taken, have 11 active volcanoes, Indonesia at least 77. Java alone includes 20, as well as so many inactive ones that no part of the landscape is without some reminder of the island's fiery past. Yet for all the awe and fear they inspire, the volcanoes of the region are essentially a force to the good. They may often devastate the countryside around their bases, pouring hot lava over their sides and expelling scorching clouds of dust and gases which poison whole valleys, but they

Mount Mayon, Luzon, Philippines

also perform an invaluable service in renewing the soil with their mineral-rich ashes that replenish the plant nutrients the heavy downpours wash away. So eager are the farmers of Java to benefit from this natural fertilizer that they even build settlements and till their fields close to the vent of Goenong Merapi, one of the island's most violent volcanoes. In fact, the terracing of volcanic slopes in Southeast Asia does more than indicate population density: it reflects the need of the people to harvest the ashes and hold them back until they can be worked deep into the soil.

The Shallow Seas

The bamboo scaffolding shown below, erected by fishermen off the west coast of Borneo as a support for their nets, demonstrates a simple fact of Southeast Asian geography—the amazing shallowness of marine waters throughout much of the area. In the Malacca Strait, the Gulf of Siam, the Java Sea and the southern portion of the South China Sea, the ocean floor slopes gently up from an average depth of only 150 feet to the coastline, which is actually the emergent area of the Sunda Shelf, a land mass that only became inundated in fairly recent geological time. Because of their

shallowness, these seas are tepid, with surface waters whose temperature is almost uniformly 70° F. the year round. They are also comparatively sweet, diluted by the many rivers that flow into them and enriched by the minerals swept down from the continent and islands by the rains. Such infusions of mineral nutrients encourage the growth of plankton, the basic food of most fishes, and as a result these shallow seas, which lack the strong currents and upwellings that in deeper oceans stir up and circulate the nutrients lying on the bottom, support a wide variety of marine life.

Mud flats, Bako Peninsula, Sarawak

2

When the Rains Come

No single element plays a more decisive role in the life of the far-flung realm of tropical Asia than the rain. On the plains of India, in parts of Burma, Thailand and Indonesia, where it is dry and dusty for half the year, men, plants and animals build their lives around the expectation of the seasonal rains—and when they come, they come on walls of towering clouds and change the landscape from seared brown to verdant green, from parched river bed to raging torrent. In other parts of the region, from the Malay Peninsula southward and southeastward through the great arc of the islands, steady rain throughout most of the year has shaped flora and fauna up to the highest mountain ridges.

The ultimate determinants of this type of climate which is so characteristic of the Oriental region are winds—the monsoon winds, whose name derives from the Arabic word *mausim*, or "season." There is a regularity to these winds which has long fascinated meteorologists, and even today the challenging question of just why they blow at the times and in the manner that they do has not been answered to the entire satisfaction of the scientific mind. Basically, they arise from low pressure areas created by the heat of the sun in tropical regions. Where pressures are low, air from surrounding areas moves in—and these movements are felt tangibly as winds. In the heated, low pressure areas, the air rises, flowing outward at the apex of its rise, north and south in the respective hemispheres, toward the poles.

In Southeast Asia, this "weather machine" is peculiarly affected by the differential heating between land mass and ocean. Asia is the largest of the world's land masses, and in summer the sun, blazing down on its arid interior, warms the earth to such torrid extremes that the equatorial low pressure system moves northward toward the Tropic of Cancer. This now becomes the dominant low for the season, drawing in increasing air masses from surrounding regions—and the air that pours in from the south is saturated with moisture drawn up from the southern seas. All along the island arc and over the drought-parched Indian plains this moisture-laden air, moving toward the heart of Asia, releases its burden as rain.

But in the autumn, as the heat of the sun progresses southward to center eventually on the regions below the equator, the situation is reversed. Now the dominant low pressure system forms over the ocean, and the winds over Asia blow generally southward. Chilled by the coming of winter, the continental air masses pour down across the Oriental region, flowing around the great Himalayan mountain massif, to which they bring rain and snow. Moving to the east, they bring winter to China. To India, they bring at first the most delightful season of the year, a cool, dry autumn, and then drought—the searing drought which, until the monsoon shifts again, slows life almost to a standstill on the central plains.

For all the seasonal regularity of monsoon winds and rainfall, however, local climates over much of tropical Asia are at times quite unstable. Statistics will show that the parts of the region that are most apt to experience real dryness are at the two extremes, in India on the west, and in the Lesser Sunda Islands on the eastern end. Over most of the thousands of miles of islands in-between, and in the Malay Peninsula and the peninsula of Indochina to the northward, the totals and averages of rainfall are high—as much as 436.53 inches in Cherrapunji in India, the second wettest place in the world (Mount Waileale, on the island of Kauai in Hawaii, is the wettest, with 471.68 inches). But what these figures do not reflect is the fact that sometimes, for reasons no one yet knows, the rains may fail to come at the expected time, or even that the rainfall over an entire monsoonal season may be considerably diminished. By contrast, there will be other times when, just as unaccountably, the rainfall is unusually heavy, leading often to disastrous floods.

The average annual rainfall in the countries near the equator or in the parts of tropical India bathed by the annual summer monsoon ranges from 80 to 120 inches. In the rain forest lowlands, annual rainfall, spread over the whole year at the rate of some rain every third day or so, may exceed 100 inches a year. At Mount Kinabalu in Borneo the annual rainfall, at the rate of some precipitation *every* day, may surpass 440 inches—nearly 40 feet of water every year. On the other hand, pockets of land within the Oriental region receive far less or almost no rain. Northern Ceylon and parts of eastern India receive as little as 19 inches of rain a year. In contrast to the dense jungles of the tropical rain forest, whose trees may be 150 or more feet high, these dry areas support only low, scrubby thorn groves no higher than 20 feet.

Plants and animals, for the most part, have developed innate cycles of their own relating to the average trends of climate and rainfall. Most birds come into breeding condition in September and nest through the period of higher rainfall that follows soon after with its abundance of insects and bursting plant life. All through the tropical equatorial region, plants follow reproductive cycles geared to the average trends: some even ripen twice a year at the peak of each monsoonal season. The most notable example of this is the durian, the spiny, noxious-smelling fruit about the size of a football which is a favorite not only of man, who occasionally cultivates it, but of the orangutan, which relishes the wild varieties. But there is no rule to describe the flowering habits of all the trees, many of which follow bizarre schedules of their own. Within a single species some individuals will bloom and fade once a year, but not all at the same time. Others may be continuously in bloom, with one branch coming into flower as another withers. Certain species bloom at extremely odd intervals, every two years or every six years. We do not know why this is so but can only speculate on possible advantages to the plant—i.e., irregular or partial flowering may increase their chances of survival under the pressures of predation and drastic weather changes.

Migratory birds are closely oriented to the monsoon winds. The koel, a cuckoo species which comes down to the islands from the Asian continent, arrives so regularly just before the seasonal switch from southwesterly to northeasterly winds that the Malays call it *burong landas*—"the bird that calls the monsoon." Fishermen in particular listen for its loud call—a signal that harsher times are coming. And when the northeast winds do start to blow they bring with them vast flocks of other migrants from northern lands. Small warblers are among the arrivals, and larks and flycatchers, shrikes, cuckoos and more than 40 kinds of wading birds, as well as hawks and many sea birds. Nearly a third of all the species of birds recorded from the Malay islands are migrants that come with the change of seasons.

Perhaps the strangest of all the migrants is the arctic phalarope, an exquisite small wader which, instead of wading, bobs and swims on the water surface, smaller and lighter than any duck. This bird is one of the commonest nesters in the Arctic Circle, where during the northern summer it shows a delightful gray, black and chestnut plumage. For many years its southern movements were unknown. Recently, however, it has been found at sea in enormous flocks between the east coast of Borneo and the northeast end of Australia. It also descends in large numbers on buffalo pools, on the rice fields and even the fast-flowing rivers of central Borneo. Here the phalaropes appear during October in full black-and-white winter plumage. With the dying northwest monsoon they disappear to the northward again, on the way discarding the winter plumage which they so unsuitably assume in their tropical wintering grounds and which makes them so glaringly conspicuous there.

In one place in the Oriental region, a remote and little-known tribe, the mountain-dwelling Kelabits of central Borneo, use the regularity of bird migrations as an agricultural calendar. They have an advanced, irrigated rice culture and they time its various phases by the arrival times of certain species. It is time to prepare for planting when the first yellow wagtails arrive from Siberia in early September, and time to actually start the planting when they arrive in numbers a month later. Seeding, weeding and bundling revolve around the appearance of a shrike from central Asia in November, a sparrow hawk from Japan in early December, and the dusky thrush, which arrives in vast flocks from Manchuria in January. The harvest must be in by March, when the last

HERALD OF THE MONSOON

The crimson-eyed koel, considered a harbinger of the monsoon in parts of Southeast Asia, is one of the few birds able to outsmart the crow. The female of this cuckoo species rids the crows' nest of its eggs, deposits her own there and leaves the crows to rear her offspring. Less cuckoolike than this behavior is the koel's cry, a rising whistle which seems to say "you're ill, you're ill" through the hot days and nights that precede the coming of the cool, water-laden northeast winds.

of the local migrants appears—the beautiful, long-tailed munia, a finch, with its striking markings of green, scarlet and blue. This little grain eater lives only for rice, wandering to descend upon the rice paddies and, if they have not been harvested, stripping the entire crop.

As well defined as the monsoon winds may be in most of tropical Asia, the climate as it affects life from day to day over most of the region gives the appearance of an almost changeless stability. Temperatures have a very narrow range. From the equator north to Ceylon and Malaysia and the southern Philippines the range of mean monthly temperatures is less than five degrees. It does not vary more than 10 degrees north to central India, and even up to the Himalayas and China it varies no more than 30 degrees. Furthermore, as far as scientists have been able to determine, these general conditions have prevailed for a very long time. There is reliable evidence that during the Eocene and Oligocene, the warm periods of the Cenozoic Era, the tropics were only about 14°F. warmer than they are today, and even this slight change took place slowly over a span of 30,000 years. We also know that at the height of the ice ages in the Pleistocene, when other parts of the world were sheathed in immense glaciers, the equatorial tropics cooled only by 1.44°F.

RAIN, FROGS AND TOADS

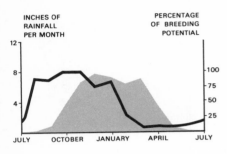

INCHES OF RAINFALL PER MONTH

PERCENTAGE OF BREEDING POTENTIAL

AFRICA

In the tropics, where the weather is almost always warm, frogs and toads may breed whenever there is enough water in which to lay their eggs. In Africa (chart above), with its dry as well as wet seasons, the toad Bufo regularis has its highest breeding potential (black line) just before the heaviest rains of the year (colored area). This enables the eggs to hatch in the more hospitable wet season. The continuously high rainfall in Sarawak, by contrast, does not limit the frog Rana erythraea but gives it the ability to breed at any time during the year.

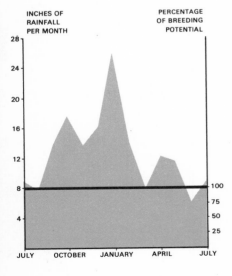

INCHES OF RAINFALL PER MONTH

PERCENTAGE OF BREEDING POTENTIAL

SARAWAK

THE result of these almost undeviating conditions of heat and high humidity has been a very stable plant life, primarily in the form of forest in which great varieties of animals, from insects to large mammals, proliferate. Forest growth is strongly influenced by temperature and rainfall: where tropical rain forest develops, the mean annual temperature usually averages around 78°F., with the mean for the coldest month rarely going below 77°F. In the Philippines, for example, the mean annual temperature at sea level is 80.2°F. In Indonesia it is 77.9°F., and similar figures apply over most of Malaya and the Indochinese peninsula. Humidity in all these areas, even in the dry season, usually ranges about 80 per cent.

The reaches of tropical Asia, the thousands of miles of mainland ranging from India through south China, are dissected by alternating ranges of hills and mountains interspersed with stretches of plain and huge watercourses. An example of a particularly confusing area is northern Burma. More than a thousand miles north of the Andaman Sea, up the Irrawaddy River, lies Myitkyina, at an altitude of less than 600 feet above sea level, with a steaming 85°F. temperature, humid and moist, with forest—what little is left of it after man's slash-and-burn tactics—of heavy, closed rain forest type. And yet within 25 airline miles rise mountains over 8,000 feet high. Here snow may fall in the winter at elevations as low as 6,000 feet. One day the Irrawaddy will probably wipe the little town off the face of the earth. At lower water the river is 600 yards wide with a gentle current. In monsoon flood, almost overnight, the width may increase to 1,000 yards, the river may rise 30 feet and the current exceed five miles an hour. Huge trees float off downstream, bridges and ferries are carried away, occasional dikes breached and low-lying crops destroyed, villages are washed out, and carcasses of cattle and occasionally even elephants float downstream. Every monsoon, dozens of huge rivers across the map of southern Asia are similarly in spate, wreaking havoc over the low-lying flood plains.

Sometimes earthquakes or soil avalanches compound the disaster. In August 1950 on the verge of a trip into the eastern Assam hills to study birds, my wife and I awoke one night in our hotel room at Shillong, the capital of the state, to hear that muffled, subterranean, grinding-teeth noise which is an earthquake.

The beds, the walls, the floor were shaking. I switched on the light. The single naked bulb in the center of the room was swinging like a pendulum. We could barely stand upright as we hurried toward the doorjamb, clutching the walls for support. We were unhurt, but 250 miles to the northeast up the Lohit River valley, several square miles of land overburdened and loosened by the rains avalanched down the steep mountain sides, killing over 1,000 Mishmi tribespeople, destroying scores of small villages and damming up the torrential river into a series of lakes in the narrow valleys.

Soil avalanches like this one are not often thought of as important in natural history terms, but they play an especially important role in Southeast Asia. A peculiar combination of circumstances is responsible for this. First of all, this is a region where rainfall is erratic and extremely heavy, often several inches in a few hours. This rain percolates down through the spongy tangle of rain forest roots into the deeper layers of subsoil, where a tremendous weight of water may accumulate. Finally, the burden of water, plus the trees crowded on the steep hillside, becomes too great: the water in the lowest strata, seeping downhill as it follows the subsurface contours, in effect provides a slick under-surface on which, suddenly, an entire hillside may break away and slide, all in one piece—trees, forest floor and all. What is left is an immense scar of raw earth on the side of the hill, and a tangle of wreckage in the valley.

From the air, scores of such falls can be seen in a single valley after a period of heavy rain. In Borneo, for example, after record rains of more than 40 inches in a recent month, one observer counted 117 landslides of no less than an acre each in the course of just one hour's flight. This sort of thing, of course, is hard on man and beast alike, but in the ecology of the forest it is important: it is a little-recognized way in which an entirely new environment is often created. The raw slice of earth exposed by every landslide is an open invitation to plants and animals to come in and repopulate it. A slide area may be repopulated by quite different species of jungle plants from those that were there before.

Where landslides or men have cleared the area frequently, debilitating the soil, the jungle plants may not take hold at all and what is called deflected succession may take place—i.e., giant ferns and bracken will form a stable though artificial plant community which may not be reclaimed by the forest for hundreds of years. These occasional bracken patches are literally the only open spaces, the only breaks in the high forest canopy. But they are anything but open when viewed from the ground: the ferns, which may grow to more than eight feet high, are thicker than any of the ordinary jungle undergrowth and have stems which can give a thin but painful cut to human flesh.

ANOTHER peculiarity of the forest cover in the Oriental region is the change in the type of forest occurring in the long east-west sweep of the Himalayas and related mountains all the way to China. This change is evident along a more or less narrow belt which runs in a north-south direction from just west of Darjeeling up into eastern Nepal. Although tropical, moist evergreen forest and tropical, moist deciduous forest are both found on the eastern side of the belt, only the deciduous type is ever found to the west.

In temperate zones, one tends to think of evergreen forest in terms of pines, spruce and other coniferous trees which do not shed their needles all at once; in the tropics, the trees are "evergreens" all right, but they are broad-leaved and superficially look much more like oaks and maples than pines. They do, however, like the true evergreens they are, shed their leaves at random through the season. This type of forest is dependent on an annual rainfall of 80 inches or more which is not seasonal but spread over the entire year. Deciduous forest, on the other hand, in which the trees shed all their leaves at once, needs a definite dry and a definite wet season, with about 50 inches of rain per year. Thus it is evident that in this area of change from evergreen to deciduous forest, there is a definite difference both in the annual totals of rainfall and its distribution through the year, and that this affects forest growth right up to the tree line.

But this is not the only interesting aspect of this change in rainfall; its effects can be seen in animals too. Right here we find a quite dramatic demonstration of what is known as Gloger's Rule, a zoogeographic hypothesis which states that, in areas of increased heat and humidity, birds, mammals and with some modification insects tend to have darker plumage or darker-pigmented surface skin than races of the same species living in the cooler, drier areas. Many species of birds and mammals which live in the forest along the foot of the Himalayas tend to substantiate the theory rather vividly. Such small forest birds as babblers, flycatchers, warblers and sunbirds have paler populations living to the west in the areas of decreased rainfall. The same species shows strikingly darker populations to the east in the heavy rainfall localities of Assam, Burma and Yunnan. Many mammals exhibit the same phenomenon, notably squirrels, other rodents and some species of monkeys.

Another rule illustrated in this interesting division of forest in tropical Asia is that of the naturalist Carl Bergmann. Bergmann's Rule states that races of warm-blooded animals living in cooler climates tend to become larger than races of the same species living in warmer climates. This appears to be a genetic response to the physical fact that a larger animal has less body surface in relation to its internal volume than a smaller animal and, as a result, is at an advantage in keeping warm because it retains body heat more efficiently. In the Oriental region Bergmann's Rule is shown by the way sizes change with increased altitude. Certain warm-blooded species, such as the langur monkeys and the tigers which live high up in the Himalayas, in colder climates are quite a bit larger than their relatives living in the hot plains. Certain birds show the same size differences—warblers, magpies, bush chats, robins, mynahs and one of the nuthatches. Throughout the plains of India and again in China, there is a similar correlation with degrees of latitude. Many species of birds and mammals living year round in the plains of India south of the Tropic of Cancer tend to average smaller in over-all proportions than the populations of the same species living farther north.

Climbing mountains is especially exciting in the tropics, as the climatic change becomes so rapidly marked and with it the effect on plants and animals. For every thousand feet of higher altitude the mean temperature will fall as much as three degrees. At about 2,000 feet in the hills the forest will be just as thick but the trees lower, perhaps only 70 feet to the maximum of the canopy—reflecting the fact that mean annual temperatures have dropped to about 75°F., reaching a low of 65° or a high of 87°. The rainfall is still high, never less than 60 inches a year and sometimes over 400 inches a year. Above 3,500 feet and up to 7,000 feet or more comes another subdivision called montane rain forest, where the temperature may go down to about 60° and the maximum rarely exceed 80°F. An alternate name for the type of forest found here is moss forest, as the trees are lower, rarely over 50 feet high, with rugged, writhing limbs and covered with dense mats of mosses, lichens, fungi and various epiphytic plants which all add to its mossy look.

The moss forest is the really distinctive biome of the higher altitudes—at least until we reach the very highest levels of alpine heath scrub, which is well above 10,000 feet in this part of the world. Ecologically, moss forest in some respects can be compared to the cloud forest of South America. In fact, but for differences in species, the two resemble each other strongly. Here, not only the flora but all of the animal life changes. And in these dense, dark, dripping tangles of low trees, there is a great deal of mystery too. It is probable that there are still many unknown forms of life in the moss forests of some Southeast Asian countries, for the local people penetrate them seldom, and then not deeply.

The great difficulty in observing the animal life of the moss forest is getting a long enough view, past innumerable hummocks and hangings of moss, so that an animal can be seen with field glasses. Collecting specimens may often be the only way of ascertaining what is there—but collecting is difficult too. Whereas in the rain forest it is a matter of shooting up into the canopy and then waiting for the specimen to fall down, here in the moss forest all sightings are on a horizontal plane, with the collector rarely traveling on the actual forest floor, and all too often the specimen, when it drops, is lost forever in a crevice or thicket into whose depths he cannot possibly make his way.

The best way to appreciate the striking changes which altitude brings is to climb on foot from zone to zone. I did this once in the district of Atjeh in north Sumatra. The lowland rain forest here is immensely tall—I walked along the trunk of one fallen tree for 186 feet before the top branches became too closely grown to allow me to go farther. It was in this forest, sitting one morning on a mossy rock in intense cool silence beside a small stream, that I saw my first orangutan, an elderly gentleman who never saw me, so intent was he on proceeding at a snail's pace through the treetops. His russet-brown hair was grizzled round his face, giving the impression of a straggling beard. He hunched as he walked slowly, almost totteringly with bent knees, along a horizontal branch, holding onto twigs to keep his balance. He seemed to be doing about as well as I would have with bare feet, walking on a branch 40 feet above the ground, and I felt very sympathetically towards him.

Up the valley road at 2,500 feet the slopes began to close in. The little stream was rushing now, trees were lower and many clumps of bamboo lined the trail. Vines hung everywhere, especially the hooked, "wait-a-bit" rattan. I saw a peacock pheasant dart across a clearing, an unobtrusive chocolate-brown creature, and my bird hunter, Layang, shot a golden cat, a beautiful, tawny, molasses-gold animal the size of a bobcat, the shape of a puma.

At 3,000 feet the valley opened out into a broad-bottomed bowl with sloping grass-covered hills all round, dotted with scattered, long-needled pines, the turpentine pine of Sumatra. The lower flat areas were filled with rice paddies, guarded against the paddy birds by withered Atjehnese crones, each perched in a thatch-hut-like nest with strings radiating out in all directions covered with bamboo or tin rattles. A shake of the string would set all the rattles going and send flocks of seed-eating finches off into the air like bees, to land in the next field. Here I saw green parrot finches, a bird not found lower down. There were more partridges, too, and many woodpeckers among the pines and dying fringe trees of the forest edges, and a fine fishing owl.

This is as high as tigers go unless they are crossing a ridge, and here a tiger had recently carried off one of the old women guarding the rice. I was implored to shoot it as a public service. I never saw it, but I came very close to the tiger or its mate soon after. I was on a saddle between two steep ridges at about 3,700 feet, coming out of dense forest toward the grassland and pine area below. I was moving slowly and carefully for I had heard a flock of babblers calling in front. The trees ended abruptly and grass drowned in brilliant sunlight lay shimmering down below, dotted here and there with a giant olive-colored pine. Just at the edge in the shade a wide "bed" of grass was springing up, stem by stem, in front of my feet. A huge animal had been lying there not a moment before. I leaned down and sniffed to get that unmistakable "animal house at the zoo" smell of tiger. Searching in the sand between the grass stems I found a partial pug mark. The tiger had moved out—perhaps warned by the sudden silence when the babblers stopped calling or perhaps because cool air from the wood had carried my scent out to him.

Farther up, where the grassland stopped and the forest closed in at about 4,000 feet, I met the monkeys. A troop of black gibbons called, their booming howls echoing from slope to slope for miles. I walked 1,100 feet up in half an hour, the forest thinning and the trees becoming lower, more densely covered with vines every few feet.

Finally, at 6,500 feet, I came into a veritable fairyland, an impressionistic *Midsummer Night's Dream*. Heavy tails of moss hung everywhere, dripping from the boles of the trees. The trees themselves were low and stunted, their branches writhing downward sometimes over the trail so that I had to duck or lunge along little tunnels of moss and fibrous roots or climb up and over branches. Orchids, ferns and small rhododendrons grew among the carpet of moss on top of the tree branches.

THREE hours and a half later I came up over a cliff edge out onto a raised plateau 9,000 feet high. This was alpine country, nearly devoid of anything except moss, with only here and there stunted rhododendrons and pines. Screens of limestone rock emerged from the moss, encrusted with lichens and clubmosses, and occasional clusters of yellow orchid bulbs like miniature onions. From one was growing a single mauve flower two inches across and sweet-scented. Clusters of pitcher plants emerged from the moss, and patches of brackenlike fern. In a sheltered valley I found a yellow *Primula*, three and a half feet tall, later described as a new species by Elmer D. Merrill of the Arnold Arboretum at Harvard.

On the highest ridges, the backbone of the whole island, I could stand in the very early morning at 9,500 feet and look out over ridge after ridge of jungle-clad lower hills, intersected with waterfalls like silver darts, on to the emerald green of the plains and finally the ribbon of the beach and dappled pale sea. The monsoon was blowing, for it was April, but it was still clear at 6 a.m. Once I saw Simalur Island 85 miles away. Puffs of cloud lay over the sea, casting leaden shadows in the early sunlight. Even with sweater and jacket I shivered, for the temperature was just above 40°F. A flock of vermilion and yellow minivets flew by into a small narrow-leaved tree, their landing shaking sprays of jeweled dew drops out of the mossy branches.

Now the clouds were heading up the valleys toward me. Thinly on the air I could hear the calls of gibbons—how many thousand feet below? A black hawk eagle circled out of the advancing cloud and then a flight of swifts went over as the clouds closed in, and in a moment I turned and ran to the tent to the sound of pattering rain.

HARBINGERS OF THE MONSOON, CLOUDS BEARING MOISTURE PICKED UP FROM WARM SEAS BOIL ACROSS THE THAI-CAMBODIA BORDER

The Dominion of Rain

Twice a year the winds of tropical Asia reverse themselves, and the monsoons are upon the land, releasing rain first over one area, then over another. The rain can go on for months on end. In some places, it converts desertlike stretches of land into seasonal oases of green, and in others, it pours down so fiercely that its fall can be more conveniently measured in feet than inches.

BRAVING THE SUN, an Indian peasant readies his field for the first rains of the monsoon, which will ride in on a high wind, accompanied by bursts of lightning and the boom of thunder.

Before the Deluge

As damp and humid as much of tropical Asia is the year round, there are parts, directly in the paths of the monsoon, that may be without rain of any consequence for months at a time. India is one such place, and as these photographs show, the dry season gives whole areas the aspect of deserts. In Uttar Pradesh, to the north, the temperature on an average day in May will climb up to 105°F., while in East Punjab, to the northwest, it soars to 120°F. even in the shade, forcing Westerners and Indians alike to spend as many of the daylight hours indoors as possible. The intense heat and glare dry out everything, burning up vegetation, reducing soil to dust, evaporating rivers. Water, so plentiful during the monsoon, must be conserved and doled out to men, animals and crops. In the state of Madras (*above*), at least three months pass by when the rainfall does not total even an inch, and all farming must be carried on with the aid of irrigation. And at Madurai (*opposite*), evaporation proceeds at such a pace that by the end of the year the land has given up to the atmosphere fully 63 more inches of moisture than it received in rain. But just when the heat is at its worst and the air seems trapped in a great glass dome smeared with yellow dust, the monsoon bursts and the tan earth freshens and turns green.

A DRIED-UP RIVER in southeast India provides living room for Indians, who erect shacks on its bed and tap its underground water, confident that no floods will come their way.

NEXT PAGE: MONSOON RAINS pelt a village in Indonesia, where downpours are heavy but relatively brief. Djakarta receives its 72
inches of rain a year in showers that total only 357 hours.

WATER DUMPED BY THE MONSOON LIES A FOOT DEEP IN CAMBODIA'S CAPITAL, YET THE ANNUAL RAINFALL HERE IS ONLY 57.3 INCHES

A Rain Explosion

Once the monsoon arrives, the rain can go on for months. The wettest spot in tropical Asia—and the second wettest in the world—is the Indian mountain town of Cherrapunji (*opposite*). Here, the mean annual rainfall comes to 40 feet, although as much as 80 has fallen in one year and 41 inches in one day—practically the amount New York City gets in 12 months. What makes Cherrapunji so incredibly rainy is its location at the end of a "funnel" formed by two mountain ranges. Moist winds off the Bay of Bengal pour into the open end of the funnel, pick up additional moisture from warm flood waters and, as the passage narrows, rise. Chilled, the moisture condenses and falls in an explosion of rain.

HER HAT HER UMBRELLA, a woman selling betel nuts sits through a downpour at Cherrapunji. The rain here rarely lets up for five months, making houses so damp that mold grows almost everywhere and fires must be lit, despite the heat, to reduce the humidity. Doing the laundry consists of washing clothes, wringing them and putting them back on—still wet.

HUDDLED UNDER UMBRELLAS, SPECTATORS WATCH A BOMBAY WRESTLING MATCH IN A DOWNPOUR. BOMBAY IS ONE OF THE FIRST CITIES IN INDIA

The Monsoon as a Blessing

In India, the arrival of the monsoons brings joy. The land is watered, the spirit seems to come back into all living things, and as a poet has put it, "Heat dies in the appeasing rain. . . ." Trees, brittle during the dry season, now support swings (*left*), which adults, as well as children, ride up into the cool air; games take place (*above*) and ceremonies honor the gods (*right*). Along the Ganges, in the wet month of Jaistha (May-June), the faithful flock to bathe in the rain-sweetened waters, believing that they can wash away 10 sins from 10 previous lives. But as the rainy

A GIANT SWING, used in the monsoon celebration of Teej, lifts children skyward. Teej commemorates the marriage of the goddess Parvati to the great god Siva.

season wears on, the dampness becomes enervating, and the Indian spends more and more time indoors. Interestingly enough, all religious festivals that are celebrated during the monsoon include fasting—a substitute for exercise.

Sometimes the monsoons are a cause of anxiety. The usually punctual rains may be late, light or intermittent, with long, dry spells in between showers. Since 85 per cent of the rain that falls on India derives from the monsoons, even a small decrease in the volume can spell drought and bring famine.

TOSSING COCONUT into the monsoon flood, a worshiper in Bombay honors the Hindu god Varuna, who controls the waters of life and is prayed to for fruitfulness.

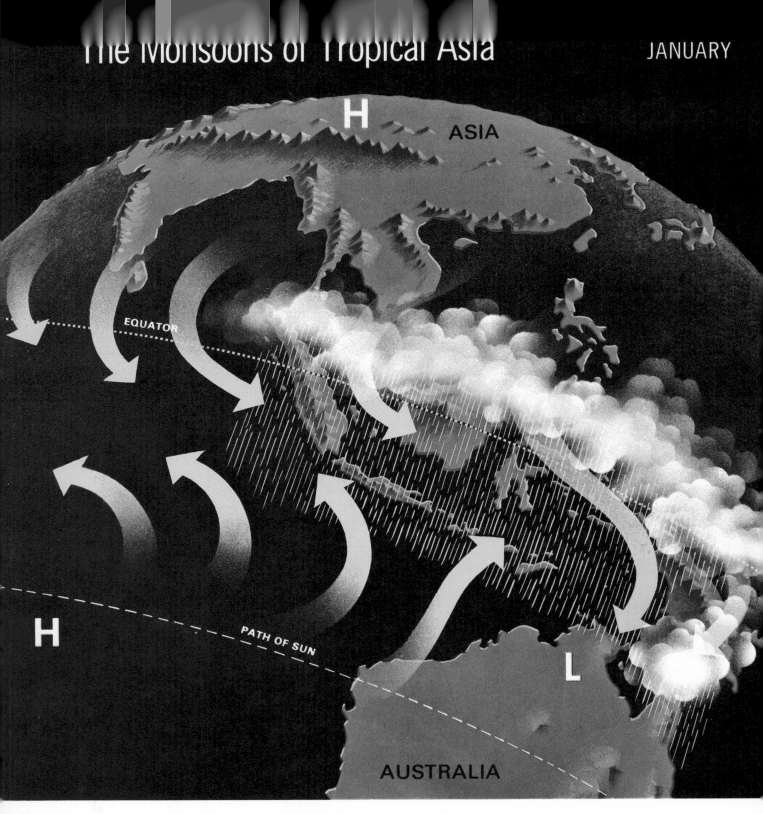

NOT ONE, BUT TWO MONSOONS come to tropical Asia yearly—a winter monsoon and a summer monsoon, each affecting the region in a different way and each growing out of a different set of circumstances. These paintings show, in highly simplified form, the basic weather picture for the months of January and July, with the broad arrows indicating the general direction of the prevailing winds.

When air lying close to the ground loses heat, it contracts, its molecules are crowded closer together and the pressure rises. But when the air warms up, it expands and loses pressure. And where cold and warm air occur close together, as over a lake and its adjacent shore, the cold flows toward the warm to correct the pressure imbalance—and the movement is wind. This is what happens in tropical Asia on a much grander scale and in a much more complex way.

During January, when the Southern Hemisphere is tilted toward the sun, central Asia becomes very cold, a high pressure area (H) forms and cold, dry winds flow out from it. These

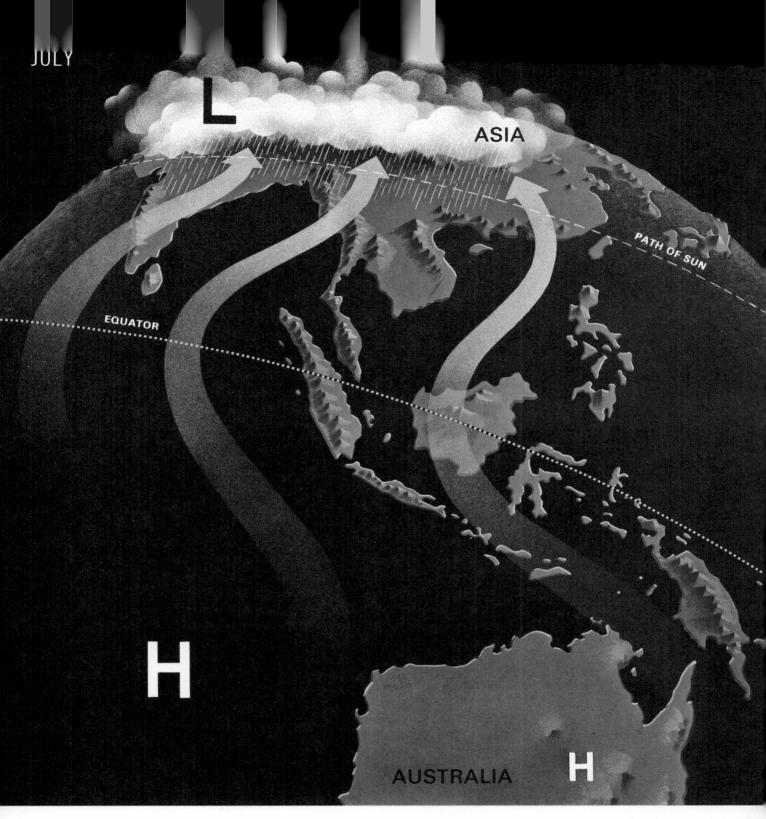

winds, joined by others from the Indian peninsula, sweep toward the equator, there to meet winds moving up from a permanent high (H) over the Indian Ocean. Converging, the winds of both hemispheres rise toward the upper atmosphere, cooling as they do, and discharge as heavy rain the moisture they picked up in their passage over the water. Because of a low (L) over northern Australia, however, some of the monsoon rains fall along Australia's northern coast.

In July, the situation is reversed. The Northern Hemisphere is tilted to the sun, central Asia warms up and the winter high disappears. Northwestern India and Pakistan, directly in the sun's path, become torrid, and a strong low (large L) develops. At the same time, Australia grows cooler, a weak high forms there, and the permanent high over the ocean, for reasons still not yet fully understood, intensifies (large H). The cool air of these two highs flows across the seas, absorbing heat and moisture, and sweeps over Southeast Asia and the Indian peninsula, releasing a torrent of rain—the summer monsoon.

SLOW LORISES, wide-eyed, nocturnal tree dwellers of Malaysia, move with the exaggerated precision of windup toys that are running down. Lorises eat fruit, insects and small animals caught with an unexpectedly swift grab of the hand.

3

In the Great Forest

THERE are three major areas of tropical rain forest on earth: in South America, in Africa and in Southeast Asia. Since all of them result from the same type of climate—high and even temperatures, high humidity, high rainfall —and have the same history of basic stability through countless millennia of time, it might logically be expected that they would all be pretty much the same in their flora and fauna. Yet they are not: as we have already seen in the preceding volumes on South America and Africa, they do have certain plants and animals peculiarly their own, and this is true of Southeast Asia too. A trip through the rain forests of the Oriental region is as much a journey of excitement and discovery for the alert observer as was his first encounter with this extraordinary environment, wherever that may have been.

Certain things, of course, will seem immediately familiar. There is the same damp, cathedral-like gloom that overwhelms the visitor to any rain forest anywhere when he first enters this world of towering trunks and vaulted canopy. There is the same background music of all the multilayered life that extends from the forest floor to the topmost branches, 200 feet or more above—the blended noises of countless unseen forms of burrowing, creeping, walking, climbing, gliding, flying, leaping life that pervade this richest of all environments. But once the eyes and ears have taken these things in, new sights and sounds become apparent in the Southeast Asian forests, and gradually this storied wilderness begins to take on a character entirely its own.

For one thing, it soon becomes clear that in Southeast Asia the tropical rain forest is by no means as uniform as are its counterparts in South America and Africa. This is a monsoon region, a place of variable rainfall, and it is also a region composed to a large extent of islands. A great deal of the region is very wet, wet enough to support the true moist, tropical evergreen forest which we call tropical rain forest; but many parts of it are considerably wetter than others, and so we find noticeable differences within the rain forest itself: differences in the types of plants that grow there, with resulting differences in the animals that live there, all of them stemming from differences in gradations of rainfall, topography and composition of the soil. And the first of these differences is between the mainland and the islands.

True rain forest actually exists on the mainland only in relatively small patches of India, Burma and Thailand. Not until we reach the Malay Peninsula, itself almost an island, do we find really extensive rain forest areas; and from here it extends farther southward across the water to the great islands of Sumatra and Borneo.

The variability of the forest cover, due to variations in rainfall, is excellently illustrated in Burma. Broadly speaking, Burma can be divided into three major areas of rainfall: a very wet region with over 80 inches annually; a wet region with between 40 and 80 inches annually; and those regions where rainfall ranges up to 40 inches but is often considerably less.

Each of these areas has its own typical forest growth. The wettest regions support true rain forest. Elsewhere, in the areas with between 40 and 80 inches of rainfall, rain forest characteristics are evident, but already there will be differences in types of trees—so much so that these are generally known as monsoon forests. Below 40 inches of rainfall, the forest covering ranges from savanna forest through thorn forest to the quite dry areas of scrub trees.

THE limitations which rainfall imposes are beautifully illustrated by Burma's principal timber product, the teak tree. Valued particularly by shipbuilders and also generally as a structural timber, teak grows best in areas with around 50 inches of rainfall and mean annual temperatures of 75° to 81°F. It also requires for its best growth a well-drained, dry subsoil. It is, therefore, a monsoon forest tree, and the great forests of commercial teak grow naturally in these areas of Burma. But because these are distant from the coast and difficult to lumber, attempts have persistently been made to plant teak in areas where it can be exploited more easily—as for instance on the Malay Peninsula. But here, in the true rain forest area, there is just that much more rainfall to make the tree commercially valueless. Teak does grow in Malayan plantations, and indeed it grows rapidly there, but it grows imperfectly, often with hollow and fluted trunks, and so it cannot be used for timber. In fact, it does not grow naturally and well anywhere again throughout the entire Oriental region until we come to the easternmost extreme, in the Lesser Sunda Islands, where a monsoon climate similar to that found in parts of Burma prevails.

The differences in types of rain forest can be pursued even further in the Oriental region. In Borneo, for example, close to the coast, on the flat, alluvial plains with deep, wet layers of soil, the so-called swamp forest predominates.

Partly the result of very heavy rainfall, partly of soil composition, it has certain flora and fauna which appear nowhere close. Floods are frequent, and the ground is always saturated. Naturalists know this as the favorite habitat of the land leech, a creature so abundant and so persistent that drastic measures are required to protect humans from it. Heavy boots and socks will not do the job: the leeches, which perch waiting on leaves or blades of grass, will worm their way through eyelets and in between the weaves of the thickest socks to get inside and bite and suck blood. Only close-woven muslin, formed into leggings that reach up to the knees, will keep most of them out.

The swamp forest has a particularly characteristic tree, the belian, or Bornean ironwood tree. Growing up to 60 feet tall, it is not one of the largest trees of the forest but it is by far the heaviest, with wood so dense and hard that it will sink in water. Ironwood is virtually impervious to decay—used as structural timbers and pilings, it appears to last indefinitely. There are reliable reports of ironwood used in stockades which showed no sign of deteriorating after 150 years. It seems to be equally impervious to insect attacks—except for the grub of a longhorn beetle, which sometimes infests it and as a consequence is regarded by the natives with some awe.

ANOTHER characteristic tree of the swamp forest is *Koompassia excelsa*, commonly known as the tapang, one of the tallest trees found anywhere in the world. Only the largest of California's giant redwoods exceeds it in height, for tapangs range from 150 to 250 feet. Their enormous buttresses may reach 30 feet or higher, tapering off into a tremendous trunk—it may be 10 feet in diameter where the buttresses end—which soars straight up for 80 or 100 feet before it begins to branch. Tapangs are a typical and majestic sight not only in the depths of the wilderness but also in areas which have been cleared for cultivation—for this tree is a particular favorite of bees, and when the rain forest is felled, one or more tapangs are always left standing as a source of honey. Alone in a clearing, they are even more impressive than in the forest, towering over the countryside like lonely giants which can be seen for many miles.

Tapangs also grow in better-drained rain forest areas and so can be considered typical of the rain forest as a whole but unique to Southeast Asia itself. Another typical tree, the strangler fig, which grows downward from the branch of a host tree where its seeds have been left by a bird, also has relatives in other tropical areas: like the strangler figs of South America and Africa, it eventually envelops its host entirely, growing upward as a true tree to the highest reaches of the canopy.

A second type of Oriental rain forest is the hill forest, farther inland and, as its name implies, growing up the ridges of low hills. Though typical lowland (below 1,000 feet) tropical evergreen forest, it too has certain special qualities which set it apart. For one thing, depending on the steepness of the slope, its canopy may be broken, because the trees are staggered up the hillside one above the other. Thus, by contrast to more level lands, sunlight in many places reaches the forest floor. Temperatures show greater daily fluctuations, and undergrowth is often heavy, with low herbs growing up to a foot high, woody shrubs up to 10 feet, and with several varieties of herbaceous plants and large patches of wild ginger. A particular menace to humans and animals alike is the "wait-a-bit" rattan, whose leaves end in a long, thin, drooping midrib set with many small, sharp, recurved hooks. Once snagged, these bite deeply into fur and clothing, and the only way to get free is to back up and unhook the barbs.

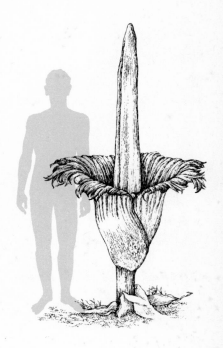

A FOUL-SMELLING GIANT

As repulsive smelling as it is huge, the rare Amorphophallus titanum of tropical Sumatra has a central spike that grows eight feet high, while its leaves open to form a massive cauldron more than four feet across. Because of its foul stench of rotting flesh, this plant is often called the corpse flower. The oppressive smell serves it well, however, by attracting carrion beetles. Incapable of fertilizing itself, although it bears both male and female flowers (below), it depends upon the beetles to carry pollen from the male flowers of one plant to the female flowers of another, assuring cross-pollination.

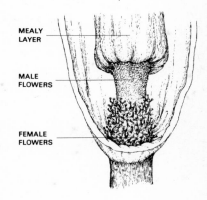

MEALY LAYER

MALE FLOWERS

FEMALE FLOWERS

108'

25'

RAIN FOREST CLIMATE

To a visitor in the tropical rain forest, it seems always the same: uniform heat and endless, stifling humidity. But this is true only on or near the ground. High in the tops of the trees, where the sun comes and goes, breezes blow and moisture being transpired by the leaves has a chance to be carried away, the swings in temperature between day and night are as much as 15°, whereas the humidity may vary by nearly 25 per cent. The graphs opposite show these differences, the upper ones keyed to the black 108-foot line, and the lower ones to the colored 25-foot line in the drawing above.

Least common but in some respects most curious is the heath forest, a type of rain forest that grows on almost pure sand. Here the type of soil limits plant species severely. Heath forest is still true rain forest but it has fewer buttressed trees, and these are generally smaller and very even in height. Flying over parts of Sarawak or southeast Borneo, where heath forest is found, one has the impression of a canopy almost carpetlike in texture.

For all of these internal differences, however, the rain forest of the Oriental region shares with that of other tropical areas the basic characteristic of a tremendous diversity of forms, both plant and animal. There are certainly more than 1,500 species of vertebrate animals in the Southeast Asian rain forests, and doubtless well over 150,000 invertebrates. As for plants, their varieties often verge on the unbelievable. Sumatra and Borneo, for instance, have some 3,000 species of large trees alone—trees with trunks a foot or more in diameter—belonging to 450 genera. Malaya has about 2,500 different trees of similar size. In two four-acre plots in Malaya, 197 and 227 tree species respectively were once counted; a single acre of Malayan rain forest is likely to have 40, 50, even 60 separate species of trees growing in it. The number of different shrubs, herbs, epiphytes, fungi and other plant forms may never be known—new species are constantly being found and classified.

I T is the trees, then, that dominate the rain forest. It is the trees, forming the canopy high above, which determine the climate close to the ground, filtering light and wind to the life below. The degree to which the climate is affected is astonishing: 100 feet up, humidity will drop from 95 per cent, its fairly constant nighttime figure, to 60 per cent as the sun rises and gradually warms the forest through the early morning, while the temperature will climb from a nighttime low of 72° to 90°F. or more by midday. But on the ground, night and day, the humidity will stay around 90 per cent for many days on end and seldom drops below 80 per cent even on the sunniest middays, while the temperature itself varies scarcely more than eight or 10 degrees. Thus within 100 vertical feet of distance, two distinctly different climates prevail in the same area, and this is true everywhere where the canopy remains unbroken.

It is this layering of climate which most significantly affects life in the rain forest. Animals show this: in the swamp forest all the creatures that stay on the ground have thin skins, like the land leeches, frogs, toads and flatworms, because the unvarying high humidity and high temperatures require only a minimum of protection. Furthermore, in this wettest of rain forests these creatures are active throughout the day; they do not need to take shelter from the sun's drying rays. In better-drained forests the more sensitive of these same animals will turn nocturnal, creeping into moist retreats at dawn when, with the rising sun, the humidity begins slowly to decrease. In the trees, meanwhile, significant adaptations to a drier life are found: skins become thicker and more leathery, and climbing and gliding aids appear as constant dampness becomes less vital than increased mobility in the branches.

Plant life is obviously affected too. Where an unbroken canopy covers the forest, only the seedlings of the big trees and certain shade-tolerant vines and herbs can develop and grow on the ground below. But once the canopy is broken, as in a cleared area, there is a significant change in vegetation due to the change in climate now that sunlight and wind can penetrate to the forest floor. Now the seeds of the shade-adapted plants can no longer germinate, and an entirely different set of plants moves in—grasses, shrubs and a confusion of undergrowth. This is probably one of the reasons why rain forest, once cleared, is so slow to recuperate—"jungle" may be quick to claim the cleared places, but it is a different kind of jungle, and not until dampness and shade are available again will the big trees slowly take over once more.

Much of the animal life in the rain forest, as noted earlier, is unseen to the visitor when he first approaches it, and this is true of the more spectacular phases of plant life too, such as flowering and seeding. Flowers are few and far between, yet they are there, hidden for the most part high in the upper or topmost branches. Many rain forest trees, in fact, flower and fruit virtually the whole year around. The hugely abundant varieties of fig do this. One common tree, *Adinandra dumosa*, begins to flower when it is two to three years old and continues to do so almost uninterruptedly for the next 100 years or more, by which time it is 50 feet high. Another tree, *Dillenia suffruiticosa*, flowers at 18 months and carries on for 40 to 50 years.

These trees, when still in the seedling stage, may be seen flowering close to the forest floor, but with other species it is far more a matter of luck, and botanists in the rain forest are presented with real problems. How to find the flower of a tree whose branches are lost in the dim confusion of the canopy far above? As the 18th Century Scottish naturalist H. O. Forbes wrote:

"The great forest trees are too high for one to be able to see whether they bear fruit or flowers. It is only on rare occasions that he alights on a grand specimen, whose top is a blaze of crimson or gold. . . . Of the great mass of lower vegetation nothing is seen but green foliage. Hours and hours, sometimes days even, I have traversed a forest-bounded road without seeing a blossom gay enough to attract attention."

Since Wallace's day botanists have been attacking this problem of finding and collecting specimens in various ways. A favorite method used to be to simply cut down trees, but this was as wasteful as it was time-consuming. Far better was the use of native climbers, sending them up the trees to explore the unseen environment so high above. The Dayaks of Borneo proved to be particularly adept at this: a fast Dayak climber can progress from a small tree to successively larger ones and finally to the lower branches of a real forest giant as nimbly as any monkey, climbing 100 feet or more in minutes. For that matter, even monkeys have been trained to throw down fruits and flowers.

Today, helicopters offer an entirely new way of exploring the forest from above. Though even these are not the ideal sky-borne platform from which the botanist can reach down and pick the specimens he wants, helicopters at least provide a way of spotting fruits and blooms and collecting data in a wholesale fashion never possible before. The tapang, for instance, flowers only once in 25 years, and there are others which have never been observed to flower—but who can say that this was not simply because a flower-hunting botanist, unable to survey whole stretches of the forest from above, was never at the right spot at the right time to see it?

Life in the trees of the rain forest offers an enormous variety of opportunities to animals, and a great many different kinds have taken the fullest possible advantage of the situation. Food is no problem in an environment which has fruits, flowers, leaves, twigs and plant debris abundantly available all through the year. No one has ever been able to count the number of species of insects which live on this marvelous food supply, flying, leaping, crawling and tunneling throughout all the different forest habitats, and very likely no one ever will

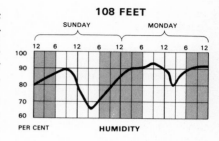

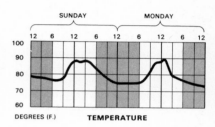

Measurements in a Sarawak forest are plotted on these graphs. Above are humidity and temperature readings over a two-day period at the 108-foot level. With sunlight hitting the treetops, the temperature rises perceptibly in daytime and falls at night (shaded sections of graph), and there is an even greater change in humidity. At the 25-foot level (below) scarcely any sunlight penetrates, and temperature variation between noon and midnight is a mere 8°. Humidity stays at nearly 100 per cent because there is no breeze to carry away moisture constantly being emitted by the vegetation.

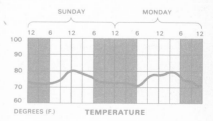

—their different forms number in the hundreds of thousands. But of other animals, some figures are available. There are, for example, 89 species of frogs in Borneo alone; the state of Texas, by comparison, harbors 33 in an area of equal size. There are 134 species of Bornean snakes as compared to 57 in Texas, a place known as pretty good snake country. There are 552 species of birds, and North Borneo alone has 120 species of mammals—a conservative estimate of mammal species throughout the Oriental region would probably be around 300. All in all, the vertebrate animals of the Southeast Asian rain forest probably total well over 1,500, which includes 213 snakes, 148 lizards, 182 frogs and 351 fishes known and classified.

The vertical structure of the forest has led to several arboreal adaptations which are entirely unique to the Oriental region. Since each of the different strata has its own climate, it also has its own particular group of specialists. Among mammals, for example, is a tree shrew, *Tupaia tana*, which never goes into the trees but lives only on the ground, leaving the higher altitudes to its various relatives who can be found in varying forms all the way up to the top levels. Similarly, there are some frogs, like those of the *Rhacophorus* group, which seldom if ever leave the trees, least of all to go into the water. Butterflies in the rain forest live in a world almost without wind, and so can afford to have larger wings and finer powers of flight than their cousins elsewhere. Most of them are found high up, where trees and vines have their flowers—from a tree platform 80 or 100 feet high they are more conspicuous than birds. But more startling than any of these is the way in which locomotion through the air, in the form of gliding, has been adopted by creatures one would never associate with any form of flying.

T HERE are three reptiles—two groups of lizards and a snake—which have developed true gliding adaptations, and one frog which is now known to have, although this was the subject of some controversy for a long time. The most accomplished gliders are lizards of the genus *Draco*, ranging in size from five to over 10 inches long. So well can these creatures soar from tree to tree that they may be mistaken for butterflies—the more so because in flight most of them are brightly colored, although on landing the colors immediately disappear and the lizard seems to melt away into the bark of the trees.

This is because the "wings" of the *Draco* fold and unfold like a fan. Depending on the species, five or six pairs of ribs extend outside the body in the form of rods, forming the ribs of the fan; between them stretches a brightly colored membrane of skin. In *Draco volans*, one of the smaller species, this skin is bright blue below, black with bright orange spots above in the male. In flight, the fan is stretched taut, and the lizard glides extremely well. Upon landing, the ribs fold backward on hinges at their base and the fan disappears, lying closely along the side of the body.

Draco volans has a brightly colored pouch under its chin which, likewise actuated by cartilage rods, can be rapidly flicked in and out, apparently as a signal to other males to stay away from its territory and as a courtship display. Often, when a *Draco* is on a tree, this little "flag," yellow in the male, bluish and smaller in the female, is the only sign of its presence, so perfectly is the rest of its body camouflaged. The *Draco* is found on the ground only at egg-laying time, when it deposits its small, round eggs in mold at the base of a tree; the rest of the time, it is completely arboreal.

The other gliding lizards are members of an entirely different family, the

GLIDERS ALL

Here are five of the many arboreal gliders of the Malayan forest, their gliding surfaces shown in color. The skin flaps of the colugo are the most extensive of any known gliding animal and enable it to travel 210 feet with a drop of 40 feet—a shallow angle of only 11°. The giant flying squirrel is probably somewhat less efficient, as is Draco, the flying lizard, which depends on half a dozen extra-long skin-covered ribs on each side of its body to give it gliding surface. The flying gecko has much smaller side flaps, webbed feet and a flat tail, and can achieve only short glides at a steep 45° angle. The flying frog is more of a parachutist, its large webbed feet slowing its rate of fall after bold arboreal leaps.

COLUGO

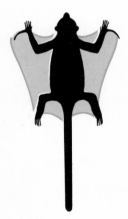

GIANT FLYING SQUIRREL

friendly and familiar geckos. Like the *Draco*, they are natives of the Malay Peninsula, where they appear in two species. They also have an entirely different gliding mechanism, which is not quite as efficient as that of the *Draco*, since it is not under muscular control, but nonetheless permits them to glide at an angle of better than 45°. More a parachute than a fan, this consists of an outgrowth of thick skin on each flank, which normally curls around the belly, almost but not quite meeting underneath—as the British naturalist M.W.F. Tweedie describes it, "a little as if the lizard were wearing a waistcoat, fitted in its younger and slimmer days, and no longer susceptible of being buttoned up." Similar but smaller skin folds appear on each side of the head and tail, and there are broad webs of skin between all fingers and toes. In flight, these webs are fully extended as the lizard dives outward; the air pressure of its fall then forces the skin folds apart and the "parachute" opens.

A minor but fascinating aspect of the flying gecko is the manner in which the gliding adaptation on its tail regenerates if it loses its tail. In the original, the skin fold is scalloped, with each scallop corresponding to one of the vertebrae which form the tail's bony structure. However, since the new tail has no bone but is built up entirely on cartilage, the skin folds which form along with it show no scallops, but a smooth, unbroken edge.

DRACO

E VEN more extraordinary than the flying lizards are the gliding snakes of the Colubridae family. These have no "wings" of any kind, but simply stiffen their bodies in a straight line, at the same time hollowing their ventral surfaces—sucking in their stomachs, so to speak—in such a way that they trap air beneath them. Their flight could hardly be called a glide, but it is definitely a controlled fall at a steep angle. These snakes are real triple-threat athletes —not only can they take to the air but they are also astonishingly fast climbers and very good swimmers.

The flying frog is a famous creature whose reputation for years rested chiefly on an account by Wallace, who termed it "The Flying Frog of Borneo." A member of the large and variegated genus *Rhacophorus*, this big, green species is entirely arboreal and does not even enter water to breed. Nonetheless, its feet show greatly elongated and fully webbed fingers and toes, and it has in addition a membrane on each foreleg similar to that of the flying gecko. Wallace never actually saw one fly; his account was based on the tale of a Chinese workman who brought him a specimen which, he said, "had come down in a slanting direction, from a high tree, as if it flew." So the evidence for the frog's gliding ability was circumstantial—but in an arboreal animal, its webs and skin folds would seem useless except as a flying adaptation.

FLYING GECKO

The most recent observations of the flying frog make of this creature more a parachutist than a glider. The naturalists D. Dwight Davis and Robert F. Inger, of the Chicago Natural History Museum, have found that the frog, on being released from a high place, immediately flings out its arms and legs as though it were crouching in the air, holding them rigidly and spreading webbed fingers and toes wide. The fall is almost vertical but braked by the parachute action of the webs and membranes. The posture during the fall is so unfroglike that it can only be interpreted as an attempt to use the air as a cushion—any other frog, in a long jump, straightens the body and limbs in a streamlining fashion which is quite different and serves a different purpose.

FLYING FROG

Flying mammals are numerous in all types of Oriental rain forest. There is a profusion of bat species all the way from India to South China, and Malaya and the Greater Sunda Islands have a number of truly odd-looking and obviously highly specialized bat types. Weirdest of all these is probably the naked bulldog bat, an almost hairless animal with long, narrow wings which, at rest, fit into flaps of skin on the sides of the back (these same flaps also shelter the mammary glands in the female). Not only do these creatures look hideous, they also smell noxiously and are parasitized by wingless flies and, occasionally, an earwig which normally feeds on the dead bats which have fallen to the floor of the caves where the colonies roost.

Besides flying bats, there are two other types of gliding mammals, the flying lemurs and a number of flying squirrels. The latter have their counterparts elsewhere in the world, but flying lemurs—or, more properly, colugos—are an Oriental region special: they appear nowhere else. Colugos are about the size of the common house cat but a surprising greenish-gray in color. Their flying equipment consists of extensible, fur-covered layers of membranous skin stretched between the neck and forefeet and on back along the flanks all the way to the hind limbs and tail. They are nocturnal or crepuscular creatures, hunting at twilight, feeding on insects and fruit. Colugos can glide at least 200 feet, and mothers carry their young in the glide.

Of flying squirrels, there are 14 species in Borneo alone, and perhaps two dozen species in the entire Oriental region. The largest of these, *Petaurista petaurista*, is an astonishing creature—fully extended in flight, it is nearly three feet long, with a tail at least as long as its 16-inch body. Seeing one of these animals go sailing down a hillside at dusk is a memorable experience, for *Petaurista* is not only big but has a rich fur of a glowing, reddish-cinnamon color which makes it one of the most beautiful of creatures. To stretch the greatly expanded skin membranes along its sides to their fullest extent, some of the large flying squirrels have a spurlike length of cartilage arising from their wrists, which they can extend like the boom of a sail.

We thus have a situation in the Oriental rain forest where reptiles and amphibians and two entirely different types of mammal have locally evolved gliding adaptations. What is the purpose of this highly specialized development arising in such varied groups? It has often been suggested that it has to do with life in the canopy—but not all of these animals live that high up. Some of the flying squirrels do, but the flying lemurs are characteristic of the lower levels, and the flying lizards, though they live in the trees, lay their eggs on the ground. Anyway, none of these creatures would have to be able to glide to live in the canopy—they are all equally adept at climbing too.

Another suggestion is that gliding evolved as a method of quick escape. However, most of these vertebrate flyers are nocturnal, and there is in any event no evidence that they have any special enemies. Nor is there evidence that their gliding adaptations have made them any more successful than other nonflying mammals, reptiles or frogs.

The British naturalist Tom Harrisson has recently come up with a new idea —that the gliding habit developed long ago, under different conditions from those prevailing today, at a time when there were more predators on the forest floor and when heavy rainfall or changes in water level often submerged the terrain for long periods. Under such conditions, gliding could have proved a real advantage in getting from one tree to another. Nonflyers must either go up into the branches of the canopy or down onto the ground to get from tree to tree—gliders simply sail across the gaps.

A SNAKE IN THE AIR

An arboreal snake that takes to the air is the subject of some controversy among natural scientists. Popularly called a flying snake, Chrysopelea coils over a tree branch (above) before launching itself. Once in the air, it draws in its belly, slightly splaying the ribs (center with detail below). The concave undersurface traps a cushion of air, like a parachute, giving the snake buoyancy. Although one specimen was seen sailing 55 yards down a slope from a tree 40 feet high, doubters claim that it cannot assume the necessary concave shape when its stomach is filled with food or if the oviducts are replete with eggs. They maintain that the snake simply hurls itself powerfully from the tree, falling to the ground without injury.

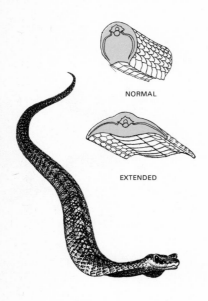

NORMAL

EXTENDED

The most spectacular way of moving through the rain forest is by all odds that used by the gibbons—the arm-over-arm method called brachiation. With their extremely long forearms, these incredibly agile creatures swing from branch to branch in the quintessence of artistry, sometimes at great speed. A family of gibbons can let themselves down from the topmost levels to the ground in a matter of seconds, in what seems to be a breathtaking series of controlled falls and huge leaps—a bewildering cascade of bouncing forms and shaking branches accompanied by loud whoops startling to the ear. Perhaps more startling is the fact that, of all their talents, gibbons are not infallible: every now and then one of them will miss a hold and hurtle downward to death or injury. The naturalist A. H. Schultz once dissected 233 adult gibbons in Thailand and found that 28 per cent of all females and 37 per cent of all males had knitted fractures which must have resulted from falls.

In the great rain forests, sounds are of the utmost importance to many animals. Frogs call, and obviously their calls are important for locating eventual mates. Birds communicate elaborately for feeding as well as display and territorial purposes. Mammals, especially monkeys, call to locate each other, to warn of predators or to demarcate territories. One of the most interesting bird habits of the jungle, that of feeding flock associations, is based on characteristic calls. Drongos—black, spangled, starling-sized birds with long tails—are usually in the van of the flock. They call noisily to each other, perhaps attracting other birds. Gradually, warblers, babblers, flycatchers and bulbuls all join up. The little fantail flycatchers are often particularly apparent because they stay low, in bushes and substage trees, wagging and flirting their expanded tails vigorously. White-eyes—greenish, warbler-sized birds with a white eye ring—may join the flock, and sometimes larger jays or magpies. This whole troop will proceed slowly through the forest, chattering and scolding, and in the process setting up a series of chain reactions. Insects are aroused and routed out to be devoured, leaves and leaf mold on the jungle floor are turned over in the hunt, and the shaking of twigs and branches higher up produces a haul of ants or winged termites. Small mammals may be attracted by the din and take some profit along the way. An occasional snake will reap a dividend from the troop, and monkeys often join in.

WHERE it is difficult to see, it is often simpler for animals to make contact by sound. Some of the sounds are outstandingly conspicuous, like the boom of the siamang, the sweet, chuckling laugh of some of the gibbons or the monumental roaring laugh of the rhinoceros hornbill and the repeated high whistle of some of the pheasants. Most of the smaller birds each have their own special sound—but seeing each well enough to be able to distinguish its note from that of a near relative can become something of an ornithological nightmare. Barbets are among the commonest and noisiest of Asian birds, but they constantly repeat only the same, single-syllable *tok* sort of call—sometimes with nearly as much variation between individuals as between species.

On the whole, the tendency of the crowded tropical environment is for the higher animals to develop rather simple noises, repeated at fairly regular intervals rather loudly and with a minimum of music or other variations. This is primarily a development for keeping contact in a dense vegetation with so many other animals of all sorts around, each minding its own business and often making its own noises as well. It is not a setting either for complete quiet or for elaborated vocal refinement. For the same reason, there are very few good songbirds in Southeast Asia—and only two which compete with the many good singers of colder climates: the shama and the yellow-throated bulbul, both of which, oddly enough, very often live near water and eat snails.

Life in the jungle is never more exciting than just at dusk. There, within the space of perhaps 30 minutes, is packed the greatest activity of the day. Around 5 o'clock the normal clamor of daytime sounds decreases, a sort of hush falls over the forest. Then, suddenly, there is a violent burst of sound all around. It is the insect orchestra led by the cicadas, arrayed in electric blue, green, black and gray, perched individually here and there in the damp, deep foliage. The "song" is produced by a sort of flexible notched rib under the second wing, which makes an incredible, all-encompassing buzzing screech like a circular saw. The noise comes, swells ear-splittingly, then diminishes and fades away. After a while it comes again. It seems impossible that the creatures are not flying, like a swarm of bees. One expects to see a great dark mass coming with the sound, but instead it is communicated from one to the other of these creatures which take up their song in sequence so that the sound seems to fade and swell and fade again.

With the insects—for many other species add their instrumentation to the dominant roar of the cicadas—come the bats. All day long the big, fruit-eating species have roosted upside down in colonies in large, bare-limbed trees, chittering and chattering among themselves as they move restlessly and bump into or elbow one another. Now they are out, and they appear, 25 or more at a time, in pulsing flights until perhaps half a thousand of them have passed. On rare occasions, a false vampire may be seen, *Megaderma*, its eight-inch spread of wings propelling two gigantic leaf-ears, a large leaf-nose, no tail to speak of, and the disposition of a voracious carnivore. False vampires eat small birds, small bats, mice, frogs and any available insects, and it seems lucky for us that they are not larger.

After half an hour these noises cease, and the noises of the night begin. The bats have settled in the trees now, and quarrel over their fruit like fishwives, screaming and chattering. Toads and frogs peep and squawk. Perhaps there is a "pooking" tiger about, trying to move his prey. Tigers at such a time have a peculiar moaning call, three notes, the middle one ascending, repeated from time to time, ventriloquial with a strange snoring intensity which sets the game moving and calling. Here a sambar bells, there a spotted deer makes its high single note, a sort of short "pow" noise. Or the kakar, the barking deer, may bark, a "gro-ow" ending short and sharp. With me it never fails to lift the short hairs on the back of my neck when I hear a tiger hunting and moving game. I lift my head to listen, wishing I could scent the creature, my hand closing round a gun barrel or chair arm, feeling as ill at ease perhaps as the original man at the cave mouth hefting a piece of long chipped stone.

To have lived in a shack at the edge of such a forest, surrounded with trees, varied yet symmetrical, trunks rising perfectly straight like the columns in some enormous hallway to the canopy above, is a strange experience. Wallace writes of it in words that still today evoke the majesty of the place: "the weird gloom and a solemn silence . . . combine to produce a sense of the vast, the primeval —almost of the infinite. It is a world in which man seems an intruder, and where he feels overwhelmed by the contemplation of the ever-acting forces, which, from the simple elements of the atmosphere, build up the great mass of vegetation which overshadows, and almost seems to oppress the earth."

SMALLEST OF ALL HOOFED ANIMALS IS THE DELICATE, 10-INCH-HIGH MOUSE DEER OF THE MALAY FOREST, WITH A SHRILL, BIRDLIKE CALL

A Hot, Humid Eden

The isolation of life on islands often tells an evolutionary story all its own: how plants and animals have adapted to a very local and restricted habitat. Thus, in the island rain forests of tropical Asia, ranging from Ceylon to New Guinea, some very common creatures have developed uniquely specialized ways—like frogs and lizards that have learned to fly and flowers that smell like rotting meat.

A CUTAWAY VIEW of the rain forest shows its complex structure of varying environments. In the humid, shadowy gloom of the forest floor, there is little undergrowth: sun-adapted plants cannot thrive there except where a break in the canopy has been made by a fallen tree *(left center)*. There, with the sunlight let in, a dense mass of broad-leaved herbs and other sun-loving plants has sprung up. When these have grown to a certain height, the seeds of the big trees, which need shade to germinate, may take hold again; the ground plants will die out and eventually the canopy will be repaired. Next to the clearing, the stilt roots of a pandanus, or screw pine, serve to anchor this tree in the soggy soil. Under drier conditions, such roots may absorb moisture directly from the extremely humid air. Be-

yond the pandanus a strangler fig is wrapped around its host tree. Having begun life as an epiphyte whose seed was dropped in a tree crotch by a bird or monkey, it has by now let down its tentaclelike roots to the earth, and these, thickening and growing, have killed the host, and the fig will one day stand alone. The climbing palm to the right of it, on the other hand, has no such deadly qualities; it spirals in graceful loops around the trunk of a huge tapang, pulling itself up by its hooked leaves. Its host, tallest of all rain forest trees, rises 100 feet or more on 20-foot-high buttresses before branching out. Staghorn ferns and other epiphytes thrive in the moisture-laden air; lianas loop everywhere from the canopy. The edge of the forest where it verges on a water course forms an almost solid wall. Throughout, white and reddish flowers show in the treetops.

AERIAL PITCHER—SARAWAK

TERRESTRIAL PITCHER—MALAYA

Rare Parasite, Common Carnivore

So rare is the Malaysian flower *Rafflesia* that few botanists have ever viewed the bulky, foul-smelling, parasitic bloom. Only one genus of vine qualifies as its host, and in the crowded rain forest this type is not everywhere found. No one knows exactly how the comparatively large seeds of *Rafflesia* are dispersed, but it is clear that few of them find their way to a new host. By contrast, the nonparasitic, insect-eating *Nepenthes*, the pitcher plant, is found in great abundance both in and out of the rain forest. Because it gets its vital nitrates and other nutrients from trapped insects, it does best in poor soil where more conventional and potentially hardier plants are unable to compete with it.

THE PARASITE *Rafflesia arnoldi* has neither stem nor leaves but blooms directly on the prostrate stems of lianas. Its buds are cabbage size; the bloom lasts five days, then rots away.

THE PITCHER of *Nepenthes* is really the extension of a leaf which secretes a weak enzyme. Insects, lured by its color and odor, slip on the waxy lip, fall in, drown and are slowly digested.

65

LAUNCHED INTO THE AIR, THE FLYING FROG HOLDS LEGS AND WEBBED TOES OUTSTRETCHED AND, IN EFFECT, PARACHUTES BACK TO EARTH

The Flying Frog of Borneo

Since the rain forest provides a vertical as well as a horizontal environment, many animals in it have taken to the air—even, apparently, frogs. When Alfred Russel Wallace saw his first specimen of the tree frog *Rhacophorus nigropalmatus* in 1885, he concluded that its enormous webbed feet must have some sort of aerial function. For 80 years, however, no scientist saw his "flying frog" in action—until these pictures were taken in 1964. Now at last it is known that the frog's outspread foot and limb membranes act like little parachutes as it makes a more or less vertical descent through the trees.

ON THE NATURALIST'S HAND, RHACOPHORUS NIGROPALMATUS SHOWS ONE FOOT SPREAD WIDE, THE OTHER CLOSELY FOLDED

SLUNG LIKE A HAMMOCK under a branch, a colugo cradles her single young. In this position or occasionally wrapped around a limb, colugos spend the day with their yellow, night-wide eyes normally tight shut. They have no nest or regular retreat but move through the upper story of the forest, gliding from one tree and scampering up the next to glide again in

A COLUGO IN FLIGHT, silhouetted against the sun, shows all its gliding membranes spread wide. Rarely seen flying, it is even more rarely photographed—in this case on movie film.

FOUR-FOOT SPAN of a mother colugo, with her baby clinging fast, shows how big an adult grows. Fur-covered, the membranes curve under air pressure and are skillfully controlled.

A Flying Mystery

The colugo is the most thoroughly aerial of all the gliding animals in the world. It is also the most mysterious, since it has no known relatives and science has learned next to nothing about its origins. Sometimes called a flying lemur, it is actually unrelated to lemurs but belongs in an order all its own, the Dermoptera, meaning "skin wing." There are two species of colugo, the mainland one shown here and a slightly smaller one from the Philippines.

search of the leaves and fruit on which they feed. As graceful as they are in the air, they climb in quick jerks, their awkwardness enhanced by voluminous and ill-folding membranes.

69

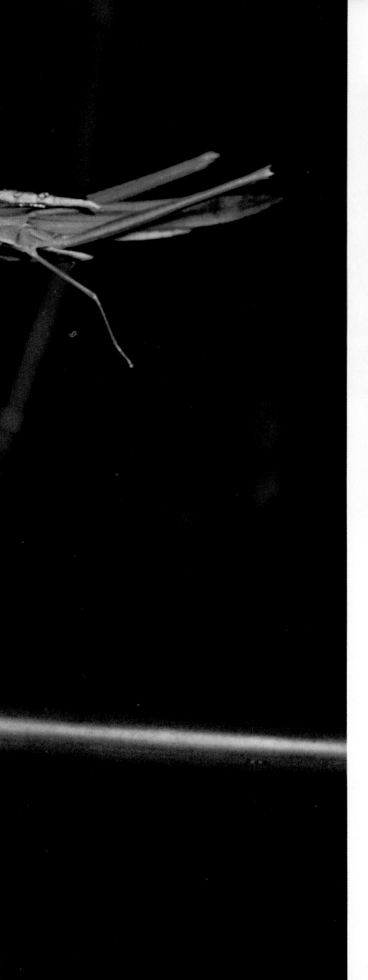

FEEDING her chicks, an oriental white-eye *(bottom)* regurgitates nectar collected from flowers. By contrast, the tailorbird sets out to hunt the insects on which she feeds her brood.

The Low-altitude Birds

The small birds that feed on insects, seeds and flowers near the floor of the rain forest build an ingenious variety of nests there. The kingfisher at the left, like its larger, river-dwelling relatives, seeks out earthen banks to burrow in, but when these are lacking in the forest, it will nest in the sides of abandoned anthills. The white-eye *(above)*, like many small forest birds, makes a delicate nest using cobwebs as a binder. The female tailorbird *(top)* takes even better advantage of the forest resources for nesting. She punctures the margin of a fig or rubber leaf with her bill at intervals of an inch or so and sews the edges together with cocoon silk to form a cone.

A FOREST KINGFISHER, just four inches long, has forsaken the diet of its larger relatives and preys instead on forest insects like the locust it is holding in its bill.

ADOLESCENT HENS of the crested fireback pheasant are modern representatives of a species which, along with the argus pheasant, for centuries provided a major source of raw material for an ancient Chinese craft. Costumes of intricately stitched plumage of adult birds were an essential part of Chinese court life. The finest feathers for this work came from Borneo.

THE CARVED CASQUE of a hornbill, fancifully decorated with peacock feathers, is the work of a Chinese artist of the early Ch'ing dynasty. Today this art form survives only in Borneo.

The Important Birds of Borneo

In the largely untouched rain forest of Borneo, the relationship between birds and men continues in a pattern set over centuries. Bornean mythology is full of bird gods, like the hornbill, whose stylized form appears in the icons of war. The Brahminy kite has strong magical powers for Dayaks; should it perch on the peak of one of their long houses, all in it are doomed. So respectful of it are they that one Dayak tribe, the Ibans, extends its powers to seven other birds that they mistakenly consider to be its in-laws—totally unrelated species like the scarlet-rumped trogon and the rufous piculet, whose behavior they observe carefully before making any important decisions. For the Kelabit tribe, which lives in the interior of Sarawak and has no calendar, the year begins with the arrival of the migratory yellow wagtail.

Bornean trade began with avian products. Centuries before Christ, Chinese traders were carrying glass beads and iron implements to the islands in exchange for hornbill ivory, ornamental feathers and edible birds' nests—the basis of birds' nest soup. The collection of these nests, produced by swifts, continues as an important industry today.

THE GREAT HORNBILL, long held in awe by natives, is as large as a turkey. It is, perhaps, the most conspicuous bird in the rain forest as, at evening, it is seen careening through the trees giving its barking call and alternating between a gliding flight and a furious flapping of wings, the beat of which sounds like a puffing steam engine and may be heard a mile away.

ROOSTING BY DAY, a host of fruit bats clusters in a large tree. Though they migrate, following the ripening fruit, they return year after year to the same tree, which soon shows the wear of the cumulative grip of their claws. Sleeping restlessly through the heat of the day, occasionally fanning themselves with a wing, they hang until sundown, when they take flight.

Fruit Bats: Dark Poachers

Just as the scent of flowers in bloom attracts bees, so the sweet smell of ripe fruit on the night air beckons the hawk-sized fruit bats of tropical Asia. Leaving their roosts at dusk, they fan out, sometimes as far as 50 miles, testing the air with keen noses. When they find fruit, they descend, squabbling among themselves, and begin to gorge in the manner of the bat below. At dawn they fly back the way they came.

Where the bats interfere with agriculture, as they increasingly are doing, they are hunted as pests. Despite this and their low birth rate—only one offspring a year—they persist in great numbers. The reasons are threefold: the bats are quite long-lived, they are relatively free of predators, and their mobility allows them to sidestep the thrust of civilization.

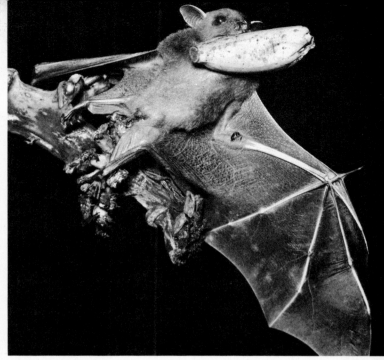

FLYING BY NIGHT, a bat carries a plantain in its jaws. Its wing membrane, stretched on long fingers, has a short, hooked thumb on its forward edge, used to climb and to seize fruit.

ENGULFING A CUSTARD APPLE WITH HUNGRY ABANDON, A FLYING FOX, AS THIS BAT IS CALLED, SINKS SHARP TEETH INTO THE PULPY MEAT

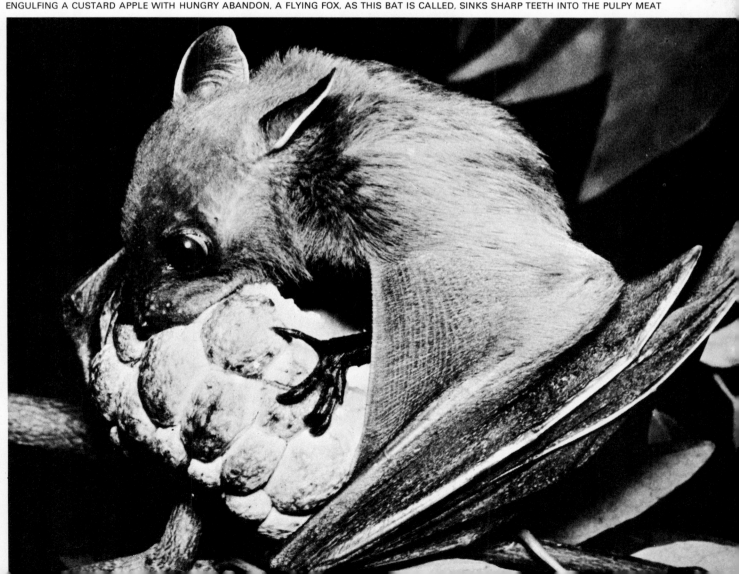

SMARTEST OF CATS, although neither as large nor as fierce as the tiger, the leopard has adapted well to the encroaching civilization of man. Though they are primarily at home in the rain forest, which best suits their nocturnal and arboreal habits, leopards also live in drier, more open country throughout Southeast Asia. There they are in close contact with farms and villages, and seem to prefer to prey on man's domestic animals, like the cow whose neck this leopard has broken, rather than on monkeys, deer and piglets of the forest. Once they have made a kill, they may return to it two or three nights in succession, dragging the carcass from one hiding place to another.

4

The Muddy
Margins
of the Sea

IF rain forest is the single most important habitat of the Oriental region, mud
is certainly the next in line. Were it possible to compile figures showing the
extent of life-bearing mud in tropical Asia—i.e., the mud of its endless coastal
flats, the estuarine mud where rivers meet the sea, the mud of its swamps
and the mudbanks of its rivers—the totals would be astonishing. No less astonishing is the life that flourishes in, on and around the mud, for here both plants
and animals of certain kinds find rich food for the taking.

But why should mud be any more extensive or important here than in any
other tropical part of the world? The answer lies in a combination of three
things: the heavy and often erratic rainfall characteristic of the area, its relatively short and frequently turbulent rivers, and the shallowness of the seas
overlying the Sunda Shelf on which many of these rivers debouch.

Violent and intensive rainfall in mountainous areas such as those which
make up so much of the Oriental region inevitably wash away considerable
amounts of soil. Even in places where the forest cover is thick and strong, landslides are frequent, as we have already seen. In cleared or cultivated areas, soil
erosion is heavier still, and in places where wet seasons alternate with dry,

drought further contributes to the erosive process by cracking the earth and loosening the upper layers of soil. When the rains come, the dried-out ground is quickly turned to mud which washes down into the valley and, sooner or later, into the rivers which drain the area.

Few of the rivers of Southeast Asia are more than a few hundred miles long —the four exceptions being the Irrawaddy, the Salween, the Chao Phraya and the Mekong. Most of them are also quite young rivers, and their short and usually violent courses keep the mud churned up and suspended, so that a great deal of it is carried out of the mountains onto alluvial plains and even all the way to the sea. The load of mud is always heavy, and it is added to still more by volcanic ash, which Southeast Asian volcanoes characteristically throw out rather than lava. Because of the amount of ash it carries, the Solo River of Java, for example, has 60 times as much sediment as the river Rhine, although it is little more than a third as long.

THE ultimate depositories of riverine silt are in the alluvial plains, where the rate of flow slows and calms, giving sediment a chance to settle, and the seacoast, where the river has its final outflow. In many parts of Southeast Asia, coastal plains are almost nonexistent—but the shallowness of the seas is such that mud flats are continuously building up in the delta areas, often at an astonishing rate. In Java, for instance, the deltas of the Tjimanuk and Solo Rivers are pushing out at the rate of more than 100 yards per year, and even the larger, less turbulent Irrawaddy and Mekong Rivers are extending their deltas at the rate of 60 to 80 yards annually.

Inland, too, mud flats may build up quite rapidly. As their turbulence decreases when they come out of the mountains, rivers tend to build up their own beds as sediment settles, and at a certain point, this causes them to overflow and change course, leaving a rich deposit of mud where they formerly flowed. Fresh-water swamps formed at river confluences or in low-lying flatlands are as typical of many parts of the region as are rice paddies—which, of course, themselves are really flooded fields of rich, deep mud.

How much of the total land area may be taken up by mud flats can be seen in eastern Sumatra, a typical place where rivers empty onto the Sunda Shelf. Here shallow, coastal marshland is the rule—so shallow that even small fishing boats must keep hundreds of feet offshore lest they run aground—and here the coastal marsh covers 60,000 square miles, or more than a third of the whole area of this big island!

Mud, then, plays a characteristically surprising part in the infinitely diverse life of the Oriental region. It is a rich and redolent habitat, often smelling to high heaven of hydrogen sulphide, the characteristic rotten-egg smell of decay. Most of it, of course, is densely overgrown with swamp plants of one kind or another, particularly mangrove, but the tidal flats are open, bubbling and crawling with life. The late Carveth Wells, once an engineer in Malaya and later a radio commentator, wrote of one of the unusual sights that the Malayan mud flats have to offer—the fish which live in the mud and walk on the land:

"Once I spent an hour watching one of these fish. I saw it come out of a hole in the ground, hop, skip, jump and walk up to a tree, climb up, and deliberately wink its eye at me! Doctor Lucas told me that once he had the same experience, except that in his case the fish was in captivity, and that he thought it winked its eye because it was dry. The fish I saw seemed to feel the heat, because after it had enjoyed the ozone, it climbed down, walked leisurely over to a pool, stood on the edge, dipped up some water in its fin and threw it over its head. I thought to myself, 'if it should slip and fall in, it might be drowned.' As a matter of fact, I was looking at the famous *Periophthalmus*."

Mr. Wells, whose enthusiasm sometimes outran his scientific knowledge, need not have worried about *Periophthalmus* drowning—this little fish whose perambulating habits have earned it the name of mudskipper can breathe perfectly well under water and, although it may not actually climb up tall trees, it can make its way up the prop roots of mangroves. Another fish which can travel over land is the *Anabas*—popularly known as the walking or climbing perch. Unlike the mudskipper, however, *Anabas* will drown if kept submerged. The mudskipper is more truly a creature of the mud, and so deserves our attention first.

Mudskippers are about six inches long when adult, neatly streamlined in a torpedo shape, with large, bulbous eyes protruding above their blunt heads, and a pair of pectoral fins which, when the fish is moving or resting with head erect, look hauntingly like tiny forearms. Any medium-sized mangrove swamp and river-mouth estuary anywhere in Southeast Asia is likely to seem literally to be ajump with these little creatures, and a camera pointed almost anywhere will get a dozen or more in a single picture.

The enormously developed, bulging eyes of the mudskippers add to their general oddness of appearance and behavior, giving them somewhat the look of miniature bulldogs. The bulldog metaphor could be applied to their chronic pugnacity, too. A pair of mudskippers, eyeball to eyeball, will adopt ludicrous defensive positions until one makes a sudden jump at the other, often knocking its antagonist over.

The mudskipper "walks" in a fashion unique to this fish, using its rather long, armlike pectoral fins like crutches to raise the forward part of the body clear of the ground and push it ahead. A broad, fleshy base on each fin and an elbowlike bend add to the illusion of forearms. The pelvic fins act in somewhat the same manner to help this walking motion; the tail at this point is merely dragged along. But if the mudskipper wants to accelerate, the tail comes powerfully into play: the whole body arches, the tail pushes against the ground, and the entire body of the fish flips rapidly over the ground. This same type of motion skips the body over water.

In the thick tangle of a mangrove swamp, mudskippers are far less obvious than on the open tidal flats, but the splutter and rustle of their movements as they slither off into the water is everywhere to be heard. For when alarmed, they make for the creek as fast as they can go. In the water, they either flip along on the surface or swim just under it, the two enormous eyes protruding like bulbous periscopes.

As for their system of breathing, it was thought at one time that these odd little fish absorbed oxygen from the water through their tails, because they are often seen sitting on the edge of a puddle or pool with their tails submerged. However it is now known that in the water they breathe like any fish, through gills somewhat less developed than in other species. Out of the water, they mix air, taken in a quick gulp, with water held in the gill chambers. When lunging for food, air and water are both expelled with an audible burping noise; the fish must then return to water to replenish its supply. Moreover, it is necessary for mudskippers to keep their skin moist—hence their habit of resting with their tails hanging into the water.

While the mudskipper is the enormously abundant air-breathing fish of Malaysia and the islands, the western part of the Oriental region and especially the great rivers of India have a close relative, *Pseudapocyrtes*, which also comes onto the land. Numbers of these fish can be seen in estuaries at dead low tide, rising stiffly erect on their tails for an instant before falling over—a maneuver apparently executed in an attempt to catch flies. Neither the mudskipper nor its Indian cousin, however, has developed anything like a lung. In this respect the fresh-water catfish *Clarias batrachus* and the climbing perch have moved further out of the water toward terrestrial living, having developed accessory breathing organs above the gills which serve as actual air reservoirs, somewhat analogous to lungs.

The climbing perch is like a fish on its way to the land. It moves from pond to pond using its pelvic fins as props, assisted by vigorous pushes from its tail. On the land, climbing perch will eat earthworms, and may themselves be snapped up by a crow or a hawk if caught in the daylight hours. Whether they actually climb trees is a moot point; it would be hard to see why they should do so. But they are useful fish to natives because a supply of them will stay alive in the market for at least a couple of days—all that is needed is to keep them in a dampened container, making sure that it is covered lest the fish climb out and walk away.

THE rich, deep mud of Southeast Asia has other forms of animal life even more numerous than the ubiquitous mudskippers, and chief among these is a wide variety of crabs. There are probably 10 crabs for every mudskipper, in fact; and while there are many species of them in the Oriental region, only two or three kinds usually occur together. Sometimes miles of mud will even be dominated exclusively by one. The crabs are so highly developed and specialized to their way of life that tiny changes in the content of the mud, the character and salinity of the water, tide flow and the microscopic plankton and other food on which they live will totally change the crab population within a matter of yards.

On the whole, crabs in Southeast Asia tend to have a very easy life indeed. The little mud crabs, most of them brightly colored, feed on the plankton which comes in fresh from the sea with every tide, sifting out the minute plant and animal organisms. When the tide is in, the crabs return to their underwater burrows to rest until the next meal is served. They have an ingenious range of devices to keep their living quarters comfortable. One genus, the *Sesarma*, bears a beautiful mud cap, about the size of a bottle cork, which is pulled down over the burrow as the incoming tide approaches.

Small as they are—too small, for instance, to attract humans—these little mud crabs nevertheless have enemies. The odd, ungainly adjutant stork may occasionally fly out onto the mud to take a few if it has had bad luck fishing. On the edges of the creeks and rivers, otters or big monitor lizards, which swim anywhere and eat anything, may turn to crabs for an occasional meal. Here, too, crabs are hunted by the long-tailed macaque monkeys, which specialize in crab eating, strolling along the banks in parties of 20 or 30, chattering and oblivious to passing boats and fishermen.

None of these predators, however, makes any noticeable impression on the huge crab population. How far the crabs have gone in exploiting the many possibilities of mud and swamp life is shown by the genus *Dorippe*, a small creature which turns up in large numbers in the Oriental region. Its two back pairs of walking legs are very much reduced in size and have turned upward, developing small, prehensile claws. Furthermore, in one of the commonest varieties of *Dorippe*, those specialized legs carry a little oval plate on which grows a tiny sea anemone. The crab sits with its bottom buried in the mud but with its claws exposed. The sea anemone serves to camouflage it, and the anemone probably benefits for its part by getting scraps of food.

The profits to crab and anemone go even further than that, however. This type of anemone has a nasty sting, which discourages any would-be predator from trying to eat the crab. On the other hand, the anemone itself would not be able to live on the tidal flats at all were it not for the crab, since the mud offers no place for it to hold onto. Once it is on a crab, however, that problem is solved —and crab and anemone grow together, the former showing concentric growth rings which enlarge its base as the anemone itself grows bigger. And if the anemone is removed, the crab shows every sign of excitement at being deprived of its partner, scurrying all over to try to find another.

Equally strange in another way are the tiny, enormously abundant fiddler crabs of the genus *Uca*. At dawn or dusk, at the outgoing tide, whole estuaries in Southeast Asia often appear to be carpeted by them, each one sitting quietly a few inches from its neighbor, the entire colony stretching perhaps for a mile along the mud flat in a belt 300 to 600 yards wide. The most immediately striking thing about them is their color—a patchwork of reds, yellows, pinks, even turquoise blue and aquamarine, while above each individual patch two little round blobs stick up—the crab's stalked eyes.

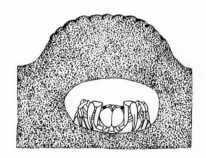

THE brilliant color of these *Uca* colonies comes almost entirely from the claws of the males. This organ is relatively enormous, just about as big and heavy as all the rest of the crab put together. On an average-sized adult, it may be the size of a pocket cigarette lighter, and it is almost always the right one which is so overdeveloped, the left one being quite small, as are the claws of the female. The unwieldiness of the instrument seems to hinder the crab in almost every way and furthermore is of no assistance in its feeding. Its primary functions are in fighting and display, and in some cases for attracting females. Visual display consists principally in jerking the great claw up and down or waving it with a beckoning motion. Males in breeding condition may seize burrows from less active competitors, usually by attacking them directly with their claws; once they have won the burrow, they will defend it by more waving or, if necessary, by more fighting. Some *Uca* species, like the yellow-clawed group, pursue their mates; others, more advanced, seek to attract them to their burrows through lively wavings of the claw accompanied by special steps. Under any unusual circumstances, such as a prolonged fight or a chase, the display color dims, the claw turning dull and the body darkening to the gray which is its normal color at rest. But even in the most savage of fights, the claw does little or no damage—it is really a feeble thing, all show and no power, which cannot even give a soft human finger a real nip.

The *Uca* claw is a prime example of how a specialized characteristic, in the absence of any deterrent such as predator danger or difficulties in the environment, can outdo itself to the extent that it becomes, as it were, an evolutionary freak. In the mangrove forest of Borneo is another example of this same tendency: the proboscis monkey. Whereas the *Uca* crab has put all of its display into its single claw, this large and powerful monkey shows it in its nose, with results which are hideous and spectacular.

Crab specialization has gone off in other directions as well in the many vari-

REFUGE BENEATH THE TIDE

To escape the wash of high tide and the predatory fish which swim in with the waves, the soldier crab burrows into the muddy sand. At the first ripple of the returning tide, this crab scurries about to form a shallow crater (top). Next it pushes pellets of wet sand up on either side (second from top) until it has completely enclosed itself (third from top). The crab then digs deeper, plastering the loosened sand above itself to form a sturdy roof. The finished burrow conserves the crab's precious "bubble" of air until ebb tide allows it to emerge again.

eties of the Oriental region. Leaving the mud flats, a few species in Borneo have taken entirely to the land—and one of them has even become a resident of the limestone caves of the islands, which has resulted in its developing a very thin shell, delicately yellow in color in contrast to the stronger hues of the outdoor types. Another crab has gone in for mountain living and can be found at altitudes as high as 6,000 feet, living in the clear streams that course through the sandstone mountains. The crabs of the family Portunidae, by contrast, have taken to the open sea: swimming freely there, they can be encountered many miles offshore, and in their aquatic existence they have adapted the hindmost of their four pairs of legs into flattened appendages that look and function very much like fins.

Another characteristic animal of the mud and mangrove environment is the horseshoe, or king crab—not a crab at all, but a king in very fact, one of the most successful creatures in the entire animal kingdom. The king crabs are actually members of the class Arachnida and as such are related to the spiders and the scorpions. Two hundred million years ago the very early evolutionary forms of that order roamed the warm and shallow seas of the Triassic; today we know them in fossil form, and the resemblance of the king crab to this arachnid progenitor is startling. Beneath its large, bowl-shaped carapace—big enough to be in common use as a bailer by local fishermen—the king crab has two rows of hard-cased walking legs, four on each side, and projecting from the back a peculiar, spiky tail. It scuttles around on the sea bottom feeding on seaweeds, young shellfish, dead fish and marine worms—a unique survivor of an otherwise extinct group, virtually unchanged in evolution during its long 200 million years on earth.

Despite its nasty-looking tail, which may be up to 10 inches long, the king crab is perfectly harmless. Indeed, in one respect it is almost obliging, from man's point of view, for female king crabs deposit their eggs, before fertilization, in dense clusters between their front legs. Children catch the slow-moving mothers-to-be, strip a few thousand eggs off the legs and often chew them raw. They taste quite good, like the less expensive forms of caviar. If the mother succeeds in getting her eggs fertilized, she digs small holes in the bottom into which she puts up to a pint of eggs, leaving them to hatch into tiny, at first soft-shelled propagators of one of the most ancient races in our world.

THE characteristic tree of the coastal mud flats and marshlands is mangrove, of which it may fairly be said that it is the plant which reclaims land from the sea. Mangroves are almost as quick to take root and grow in the silt deposited by rivers as the rivers are efficient in giving them silt to grow on, and trying to assess whether mangroves cause silt deposition or whether silt causes mangroves to take hold and develop is like asking the old question about the chicken and the egg. Certainly the mangroves' many-tangled root systems help silt to settle and hold it fast once it has, and when mangroves have taken hold on a large scale, a raising of the land level is likely to follow as more and more silt is laid down, so that eventually what was a shallow, underwater or tidal flat becomes solid ground.

The mangroves of the Oriental region total some 30 species, all of which are able, through one form or another of specialized roots, to secure and maintain a firm foothold in the soft mud. All of them, too, will tolerate, to greater or lesser degrees, both salt and fresh water, since most mangrove swamps are flooded twice daily by the tides. Some mangrove trees reach imposing heights up to

100 feet, others are low and shrublike. All are evergreens, most with shiny leaves and small flowers.

The root systems are generally of three types. In one form, the trunk sends many roots like flying buttresses into the mud, creating a truly impenetrable tangle. Another sends its roots out horizontally, and every so often each root shoots a sharp half-loop straight upward and downward again, like a knee protruding above high water. A third type, instead of looping up and back, simply sends a protuberance, like a stubby branch, up into the air. In all three cases the aerial portions supply oxygen for the rest of the root system, and as the land level rises, these special adaptations send out new processes while the older roots are gradually stifled below.

Mangrove seeds are also especially adapted for a muddy environment. For one thing, most germinate before they leave the parent tree, so that when they hit pay dirt, so to speak, they are seedlings ready to take immediate advantage of it, putting out their own roots and starting to grow. They are heavy, fleshy and often shaped like plumb bobs, so that when they fall into the mud, they penetrate it deeply, planting themselves. But they are also able to survive considerable water voyages in case they are floated away by tide or current.

It is also interesting to note that the tide, in effect, sorts out the different kinds of mangroves, leading to the formation of zones of various species along the shoreline. This is the logical result of the different species having different tolerances to salt water. Where the tide floods most deeply, right along the shoreline, the most salt-tolerant species thrive. Next in line, moving inland, are those with a somewhat lower salt tolerance and, as the silt builds up and the land rises, the ability to grow in salt water becomes less and less important, so that finally, in the farthest inland belt, a fresh-water swamp exists where salt tolerance is no longer a factor at all.

The depth of the mangrove forest along the coastline varies greatly. Along the west coast of Malaya, for example, from Kedah in the north to Singapore, it may be anywhere from a few trees to 12 miles deep—but it does form an almost unbroken fringe along the entire coastline. In the front ranks, often growing on banks which have been exposed for only a few days, is the type known locally as *api-api*, or white mangrove, whose grayish leaves are a particularly favored place for fireflies. At night, these are so numerous, large

MARCH OF THE MANGROVES

Mangrove species often create new land by taking root in the mud of the seashore and establishing a forward wall of plants that traps debris and silt. The pioneer genus Sonneratia takes hold just above the level of the lowest of the low tides (A). It can stand almost continuous flooding because its roots are particularly tolerant of salt water. As the land bank begins to build, Sonneratia is replaced by Rhizophora. The roots of this genus are lapped regularly by the various tides (B, C, D), but they too can abide heavy dosages of salt water. Bruguiera flourishes higher on the new land bank, its more sensitive roots washed only twice a month by the highest of all tides, the spring tide (E). At the far right of this schematic drawing are trees on dry land behind the advancing mangroves.

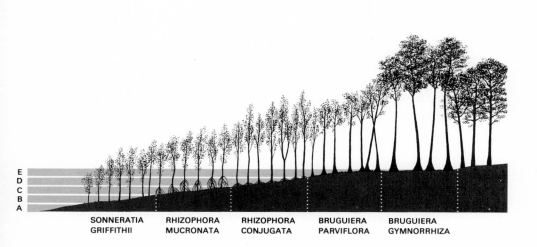

| SONNERATIA GRIFFITHII | RHIZOPHORA MUCRONATA | RHIZOPHORA CONJUGATA | BRUGUIERA PARVIFLORA | BRUGUIERA GYMNORRHIZA |

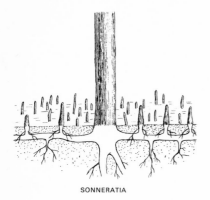

SONNERATIA

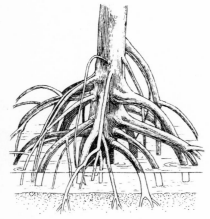

RHIZOPHORA

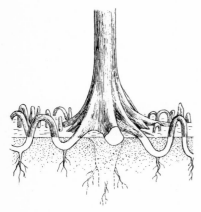

BRUGUIERA

ROOTS FOR A TIDAL LIFE

Since one of the functions of tree roots is "breathing" to take in oxygen and get rid of carbon dioxide, mangroves are faced with a problem in their oxygen-poor environment of mud and tidal water. They solve it in various ways. The genera Sonneratia and Bruguiera both have widespread underground root systems with shoots or loops which jut into the air at low tide. Rhizophora grows stilt roots that both breathe and support the trunk.

and bright that they have long since become a traditional guide to sailors.

The *api-api* is an early colonizer, one of the primary land builders in this region; behind it come, in succession, two other types, *Rhizophora* and *Bruguiera*. Farther inland, as the salinity diminishes, fresh-water species of various trees gradually take over, prominent among them the nipa palm, with which most of the huts in coastal villages throughout Malaysia are thatched, and pandanus, which provides the leaves for sleeping mats and bags.

Behind the mangrove belt lies the fresh-water world of Southeast Asia's rivers, with a wealth of fishes that tell us much about the region's past. Among fresh-water fishes, there are two broad divisions: the primary fishes, which are strictly confined to fresh water and ordinarily never enter the sea, and the secondary fishes, which tolerate some salt water and thus have been able in many cases to be distributed from island to island across salt-water gaps. It is the primary fishes which give us the most important clues to the past, for if two species of this type are found in widely separated geographic localities and yet are closely related to each other in terms of anatomy and general life habits, then it is an almost certain bet that at some point in history they had a common geographical range.

The Oriental region is enormously rich in the dominant varieties of primary fishes, including many varieties of carp, catfishes and loaches. Primary division fishes reach Ceylon, Formosa and Hainan. Most primary division fishes also reach Sumatra, Java and Borneo, although a few do not reach all the way to the eastern end of Java, showing that that end of the island, as indeed we know from its geological history, has had an uneven record of elevation and submergence of the land through the Cenozoic. Two or three members of the carp and minnow family cross from Java east to Bali, Lombok and Sumbawa, the first three of the Lesser Sunda Islands, but they get no farther. Several carp and minnow species also reach the southern and western Philippines, having presumably journeyed thither via ancient connections between Borneo, Palawan, Mindoro or east across the Sulu Islands to Mindanao. The fossil history of these fishes goes back at least 50 million years to the Eocene and may even go as far back as the later parts of the Cretaceous.

Secondary division fishes reach as far as Celebes and northern Luzon. There seems no reason to doubt that a limited tolerance for sea water has helped these, such as some of the catfishes, to cross the kind of narrow ocean barriers that separate the islands from each other.

THE most important group of Oriental fishes are the cyprinoid, or carp-like, fishes, of which several entire families of fishes are found in this region and nowhere else. This super family group—perhaps largest of all fish families with at least 2,000 known species—seems to have radiated out into other continents, throughout temperate Eurasia, into North America and to Africa from the heartland of the Oriental region. Most of the important fishes of southern Asia are in this group, including the famous mahseer of India and Burma, a giant carp which may reach a weight of 110 pounds in some of the large Indian rivers and which, if caught on hook and line, fights and flings itself into the air as wildly as any tarpon.

A fascinating variety of loachlike fishes is found only in the torrential rivers of Southeast Asia, from the Himalayas east to southern China, Java and Borneo. Many of these belong to the family Homalopteridae, characterized by a modification of the paired fins which are placed more horizontally than is usual among loaches and in many cases are broadened and flattened to provide gripping surfaces with which the fish can hold itself to the bottom. The reason for this is perfectly plain: tropical hill streams are about as extreme an environment as any fish can subsist in, combining as they do the violence of rapids and falls, and the raging turbidity of seasonal floods, when small stones several inches across may be suspended in the vast deluge like so many grains of sand. Here food becomes difficult to find, insects may be swept away, and any fish that lives must feed on diatoms and algal slime covering rocks on the bed of the stream, while at the same time anchoring itself in some fashion against the surge of the current.

Many and varied are the adaptations which have evolved for these purposes in the fishes that have managed to creep up these fast-flowing rivers of the Oriental region. Some species have the skin on the ventral surfaces puckered into grooves and ridges, either on the thorax or on the broadened surfaces of the pectoral or pelvic fins. Some have developed suckers on the underside of the head; others have adapted the whole of the ventral surface to form one large adhesive surface which is rendered still more effective by the pressure of the current forcing the forward end of the fish against the bottom. In still others the outer rays of the paired fins are heavily corrugated to provide friction against the bottom, and further adhesion is provided by the inner rays which, pumping out water from underneath the fish, create a partial suction in the corrugated fin parts.

TWIN HOLES IN THE HEAD

Fish normally breathe by taking in water by mouth and extracting oxygen from it as it passes out through the gills. This is not possible for the eight-inch mountain carp Gyrinocheilus, which must use its mouth as a sucker to hold onto rocks in swift mountain streams and cannot open it for normal breathing. Instead, it uses two holes in its head, passing water through the gills as shown below.

RESPIRATION presents special and unusual problems. In these cold and turbulent streams, leaping over rocks and boulders, cascading down innumerable falls, the water is highly oxygenated, and as a consequence many fishes tend to have gills and gill openings reduced in size. Interestingly enough, however, the gill cavity itself is not correspondingly smaller—for the logical reason that the fishes must also cope with situations when the water is not so overrich in oxygen—as for example during heavy floods when the rivers flow deep and are loaded with silt. At such times the fish can store water or even resort to mixing water with air in the gill cavity.

One of the most unusual breathing adaptations is that of two species of *Gyrinocheilus*, found in the torrential streams of Thailand and Borneo. For lack of a common name, these have aptly been called "head-breathers"—for they do indeed breathe through two good-sized openings in the back of the head which lead directly into the forward portion of the gill chamber. The mouth of these species, although still connected to the gill chamber, has completely lost all respiratory functions, since it is entirely given over to holding the fish against the current by suction and also feeding by scraping off the algae growing on stones on the bottom. Breathing is taken care of by the two head openings, which are equipped with thin flaps of skin that act as valves: these skin flaps have been seen to open and close as often as 240 times per minute, giving a dramatic indication of the fish's rate of respiration.

In Assam I have often watched people fishing for air-breathing loaches or snakeheads in roadside mud ditches. Wading into the black glutinous substance up to the thighs, the man or woman carries a conical woven basket, perhaps three feet long. Holding the small end up high, the fisherman every so often claps the contraption, open end down, into the mud and water. Then, dexterously whipping it up in a reversed position or sometimes feeling under it, he may retrieve a small, wriggling, blackish fish from the noisome interior. Even stranger fishing methods are employed in the Sundarbans, the tidal mangrove creeks of Bengal and East Pakistan, and vividly described by the naturalist Sainthill Eardley-Wilmot:

"The creeks are full of fish, and of fishermen who use nets with skill and success. They have a curious custom of training otters to their service; these animals are secured by a girth to a boom projecting over the gunwale, so that they rest on the surface of the water and can be released so soon as occasion arises. The pack then, after the manner of otters, extend in line across the creek, and drive the frightened fish headlong into the nets, when the otters are again tethered and rewarded with some savoury morsel. In open dugouts may be seen rows of lugubrious cormorants sitting awaiting the order of the paddler, and this is conveyed with emphasis as each bird is pushed into the water, to return after a time with a fish in his beak. A ring on the neck prevents the bird from swallowing his prey, so that he received for his labour only a fixed wage, and, however skilful he may be, he must go hungry till the fishing is over. There is a great fish-market at Khulna, the chief town of the district, and baskets of fish of assorted sizes, of huge prawns, and of crabs, are daily despatched in the fish-mail to Calcutta."

In a quiet way, the king of all of Southeast Asia's rivers is not noisy man, but another of the most intelligent kinds of mammal. The Irrawaddy dolphin is one of the few fresh-water cetaceans, a small creature, usually less than six feet long and colored a pale battleship gray-blue. Even in these days of outboard motors and river steamers, the graceful curving plunges and usually short, curved dorsal fin of this little dolphin are the signature of another kind of successful living, one that it pursues not only for a thousand miles up the Irrawaddy but as far as the going is good on much smaller rivers in the islands east as far as the Celebes.

THE most graceful of all the riverine animals, in the opinion of many observers, is the fishing cat. This civetlike creature, up to three feet in length and marked by even lines of dark spots on a gray background, is found on rivers on the west side of the region. Two notable birds are also to be found on Southeast Asia's rivers. One of these is the snakebird, or darter, closely related to the anhinga of the Americas, a branch of the pelican order. This bird is distinguished for its skill in spearing fish with its long beak, while most birds catch between the mandibles.

The second really characteristic bird of these rivers is the scarlet and black broadbill, a chunky, thrush-sized bird which lives largely on snails along the riverbanks and the surrounding forest floor. Most broadbills hang their untidy, domed nests. This one hangs them on branches always right over the river. One of these nests, taken away and put in a museum, is a most conspicuous object. But left where it belongs, its untidiness looks just like driftweed and grass which accumulate and bind round branches and twigs whenever the river level rises in flood. In a climate where such flooding is only too frequent, this broadbill perfectly calculates the safe level at which it can hang its nest. The water may be 20 feet below a branch when it starts building, but when the river rises, the nest will be at just the right level. Experienced river travelers in Southeast Asia always keep a lookout for the first broadbill's nest—that is their best indication of how high the highest flood will *not* reach, and that is useful information for those who are traveling long and far with valuable scientific equipment in remote and difficult country.

DELICATE FEATHER STARFISH CLINGING TO A PIECE OF CORAL LIVE IN THE LOWEST TIDE ZONE, EXPOSED TO THE AIR ONLY BRIEFLY EACH DAY

Neither Land Nor Sea

Much of the land of tropical Asia is embraced by a wide girdle of mud, a richly fertile environment that supports a highly special-ized variety of life. Fed by the silt of rivers emptying into shallow seas, this is a world of repeated immersion and exposure where the opportunities offered by land and sea have developed such unique species as trees that extend shorelines and fish that walk.

MEANDERING TO THE SEA, SARAWAK'S SANTUBONG AND SALAK RIVERS CREATE A CLASSIC MUD AND MANGROVE ENVIRONMENT. ON THE LOWLANDS

A CRAB'S-EYE VIEW OF THE SAME AREA AT EBB TIDE SHOWS HOW INTIMATE IS THE RELATIONSHIP BETWEEN THE MUD, THE LAND AND THE SEA.

IN THE BACKGROUND, MANGROVE JUNGLE COVERS THE DELTA ISLANDS, PUSHING EVEN FARTHER INTO THE FLATS EXPOSED AT LOW TIDE (BELOW)

THE 13-FOOT TIDE THAT SWEEPS INTO THIS LAGOON TWICE EVERY DAY ALTERNATELY COVERS AND EXPOSES HUNDREDS OF ACRES OF SHALLOW FLATS

A LONE MANGROVE, exposed at low tide, reveals the spidery root structure which here provides a firm purchase in muddy sand, trapping silt and flotsam that will decay into rich soil.

How Mangroves Get Their Mud

Mangroves, those ubiquitous and durable plants, are found along the coasts throughout most of tropical Asia. In some areas, they grow in such profusion that even jungle conquerors like the U.S. Army Corps of Engineers found them impenetrable. But there are also great stretches where they will grow only sparsely. The reason for this lies not just in conditions at the seashore but in the composition of the great inland mountain ranges hundreds or even thousands of miles away. If the mountains are granite, which disintegrates into fertile mud on the long journey to the sea, mangrove jungles are almost certain to be found on the coast. But if they are sandstone, the unfertile silt left at the shore will not support massive mangrove colonies. A classic example is the Malay Peninsula, whose western coast harbors a steaming mangrove jungle while the wave-swept, sandy east coast is virtually barren.

NEW GENERATIONS of mangroves live on rotting remains of old trees. The tree in the foreground has such extensive stiltroots that its original taproot has withered.

AMPHIBIOUS CRAB, GENUS SARMATIUM

HERMIT CRAB, GENUS COENOBITA

SOLDIER CRAB, DOTILLA MICTYROIDES

SWIMMING CRAB, NEPTUNUS PELAGICUS

GHOST CRAB, OCYPODE CERATOPHTHALMA

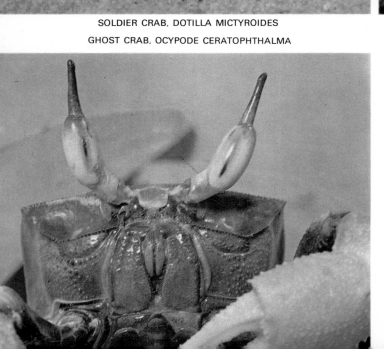

A Galaxy of Crabs

Wherever water meets land in tropical Asia, there are countless millions of crabs. The pictures on these pages are only a small sample of their colorful diversity. The great robber crab (*opposite*, *above*) spends nearly all of its adult life ashore. But at breeding time the females cast their buoyant larvae into the water, a primal instinct that colonized many isolated islands which the adults themselves could never have reached. The hermit crab (*top row*) is naked and vulnerable until it finds an abandoned shell, which then provides it with one of

LAND CRAB, CARDISOMA CARNIFEX

ROBBER CRAB, BIRGUS LATRO

BEACH CRAB, MATUTA LUNARIS

AMPHIBIOUS CRAB, GENUS SESARMA

AMPHIBIOUS CRAB, METOPOGRAPSUS OCEANICUS

the most impregnable defenses in the crab family. Malayan sand crabs are protected by camouflage: their dark gray shells blend perfectly with sandy beaches, making them nearly invisible until they move—hence their popular name, "ghost crabs." Despite all these obvious outward differences, all 4,400 species of true crabs throughout the world have several features in common, including movable eyestalks, a hard shell covering at least part of the body, and five pairs of legs—the first pair ending in claws, the others for walking or swimming.

The Fastest Fish on Land

Until quite recently, myth and mystery surrounded the life secrets of that popeyed clown of the tropical Asian mudflats, the mudskipper. Its breathing mechanism, for instance, was so little known that it was thought to absorb oxygen through its tail. Such misconceptions arose largely because mudskippers are almost impossible to catch alive, even for seasoned hunters. They can change direction on land faster than any human reflexes can react, and in water they can scurry over the surface like skipping stones, covering two to four feet at a jump. One expedition, in its scholarly report on mudskippers, devoted paragraphs to describing how a team of scientists gave chase to one in vain, lunging through the mud until they dropped from sheer exhaustion, laughing hysterically at their own ludicrousness. Another team was equally unsuccessful until it reverted to an old schoolboy trick—shooting rubber bands at the fish and stunning them.

SUNNING THEMSELVES, half a dozen mudskippers congregate on a coconut palm trunk. Though still tied to the water, they seem to prefer life in the air; here they may be alert for insects.

CRAWLING ASHORE, an army of mudskippers squirms over the mud. Their pectoral fins, used like any fish's for balance in the water, have become efficient limbs for walking on land.

FACE TO FACE, two mudskippers cling to a mangrove shoot. This species' ability to leave the water is based on several sound reasons: walking increases the chance of survival for fish that might get stranded in shrinking tidal pools; breathing is difficult in muddy brackish water; most important, food is easier to find since other species cannot compete on land.

Hunters Large and Small

Of all the predators that haunt the shores of tropical Asia, none presents a greater contrast than the archerfish and the crocodile. Archerfish are formidable in their own small way, but crocodiles, attacking man and beast alike, are feared as much in inland rivers as they are far out at sea. Most vicious is the salt-water crocodile, which ranges farther than any other of its kind, swimming in open seas from India to the Philippines and Australia. Man, in turn, preys heavily upon crocodiles: in the Irrawaddy delta natives eat them regularly, catching them on hooks baited with ducks and puppies.

AN AQUATIC MARKSMAN, the archerfish shoots down its prey by squirting water from its mouth. In the first two frames it is taking aim at an ant just off camera. In the third frame, the needle-fine jet makes a direct hit, and then the hunter waits for the victim to drop.

A MONSTER OF THE MUD, the salt-water crocodile is more feared along Asian coasts than even the tiger. The Indonesian specimen below is only medium-sized—the largest crocodile of this type ever recorded, in Bengal, was 33 feet long and 13 feet 8 inches around the middle.

5

Island Hopping

BEYOND the looming mass of the continent, like pearls strung out in the surrounding seas, lie the islands of the Oriental region, magnificent in appearance, richly diverse in their natural wonders, the constant marvel of the traveler. To sail through them is the most rewarding of all journeys in this area. It is then that their variety and savor can be realized, sensed in all possible ways. The smell of the land from the sea is exciting and piquant—the sour smell of drying coral reefs, the sulphurous smell of mangrove flats, the warm earth smells of forest after rain, the pungent smell of cinnamon groves, the tapestry of aromatic odors from a hundred village cooking fires wafted across a bay.

The islands of this region belong to three types, and for an understanding of the area as a whole it is necessary to understand something about them and their origins. To begin with, we must go back to a subject with which readers of these volumes are now familiar, since it has been referred to so many times before: the raising and lowering of the level of the ocean during the Pleistocene ice ages. Some of the largest and most important islands in the area are actually parts of the continent of Asia and can be considered islands only because the level of the ocean happens to be high today and they are "temporarily" cut off from the mainland. A look at the map on pages 18 and 19 will make this instantly clear. The great peninsula of Thailand, Cambodia and Malaya that hangs south from China actually continues on to include Sumatra, Java and Borneo, since all three are surrounded by shallow water. If the sea level should drop to where it was 10,000 or 20,000 years ago, they again would be part of Asia.

So, our first island type is a piece of continental real estate that at the moment happens to be separated from its continent-parent. In addition to the three islands mentioned above, there are two more in this category, lying close to the coast of China: Hainan and Formosa. Another, Ceylon, is just below the southern tip of India. Although none of them looks very large on a map of the world, they are enormous as islands go. The combined area of all six islands is equal to nearly 500,000 square miles, about twice the size of Texas, and their total population is over 106 millions.

In a second category, around and about these larger islands are fringing chains of archipelagoes in a multitude of shapes and sizes. Islands of this type are different from the continental islands in that they have no close geological connection with the mainland. They are not surrounded by shallow seas. On the contrary, the waters between them are deep, so deep that the most informed opinion suggests that they may never have been connected to the mainland at all—or even to each other. They appear to be separate acts of creation, the result of independent and complex movements of the earth's undersea crust in what is known to be one of the most geologically unstable areas in the entire world. Scientists are impressed by the fact that the outer edges of some of these islands, notably the Philippines, fall away into the deepest parts of the sea. There is obviously some connection between the volcanic and crustal activity that forms the islands and the deep trenches that lie near them, and many complex theories have been advanced, the most persuasive of which is discussed at some length in a previous volume in this series, *The Sea*.

The third type is the true oceanic island. This is usually clearly volcanic in origin and may consist of a single island or a peppering of peaks poking up through the sea to form a small archipelago. Some of these oceanic islands are jagged and mountainous, attesting to the enormous powers of the upthrusting volcanoes that made them. Others are flat atolls, rings of coral growing on the tops of mountains whose peaks are now beneath the surface of the Pacific.

Each of the three categories of islands—the large continental ones, the smaller orogenic ones, the oceanic groups and atolls—has its own particular fascination. In all of them natural scientists have long found living laboratories in which to study that most intriguing question of zoogeography: how plants and animals have come to be where they are.

THROUGH the years since Darwin and Wallace first made the world aware of the great natural laws explaining the origins of species, many theories have been put forth to explain the dispersal of flora and fauna through islands. Southeast Asia ideally demonstrates one of the most persuasive of these theories, the "filter bridge" propounded by the noted paleontologist George Gaylord Simpson.

Let us look at the island of Ceylon to see what a filter bridge is and how it works. This island, of 25,000 square miles and varied terrain, lies only 30 miles from the Indian mainland, and it shares with India a number of different kinds of animals and plants—but their distribution, particularly of things that are *not* where they might be, is highly significant. At the point where they are

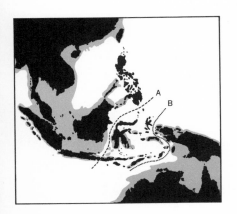

SO CLOSE, YET SO FAR

The islands of Southeast Asia have a peculiar distribution of plants and animals, there being many species in common throughout the islands to the west of line A on this map, but few of those species to the east of it. That is because all the areas shown in color were above water during the Pleistocene, and some of today's islands were joined together to form a huge peninsula over which species could move freely. This phenomenon was first noticed by Alfred Russel Wallace. At its southern end, Wallace's Line passes through the island chain at the Lombok Strait. Though narrow, the Strait is very deep and was an effective barrier. A similar situation prevails with respect to New Guinea and Australia, which also were once connected and which today share many species. However, few of these worked their way westward across deep water beyond line B.

closest together, India and Ceylon share a very dry climate. The rainfall is seldom more than 25 inches annually, and the two land masses face each other across an area of salt water, fringed on both sides by shifting dunes and almost desertlike living conditions. Was this always the case? Almost certainly not. For at one time or another the seas were lower, the two lands connected, and the climate was rainier. There was probably a continuous stretch of deciduous forest extending down from areas in which such forest still exists in India all the way to central Ceylon, which also still has deciduous forest. We know this because there are forest animals in Ceylon today, closely related to Indian types. They obviously came from India and they could have come only when a continuous strip of forest was in existence, because they could not have traveled across the arid sections that now lie between.

At other times it may have been even rainier, rainy enough to turn the India-Ceylon stretch of deciduous forest into tropical rain forest, permitting the passage of animals that could live only in that environment. It is in these changing conditions that the so-called filter bridge can best be seen to operate. Given certain favorable climatic and forest conditions, certain animals can get from India to Ceylon, but others cannot; conditions are unfavorable to them and they are filtered out. So, if we picture changing climates and changing ocean levels, we can visualize a filter bridge working, over thousands of years, to allow some creatures to thread their way down along an isthmus, spreading by way of the forest type of their selected habitat, from one finger of suitable forest to another, some species dropping out along the way but others managing to continue. Thus the leopard made it from India to Ceylon but not the tiger, the otter but not the weasel, the Indian sloth bear but not the hyena. For various reasons—the climate, the forest or the lack of it, the time involved, perhaps chance extinction or even factors we do not know about at all today—certain animals found the narrow connection feasible to cross, others found it still a rugged and obviously insurmountable barrier.

Even as the wet and dry jungles of the lowlands of south India and Ceylon waxed and waned, so the same over-all climatic changes affected the mountains. Increased rainfall, humidity and slight temperature changes helped to develop a pathway for the more temperate forms of plants and animals so that they could become distributed along the chain of hills just south of the Himalayas in central India. From these hills they progressed along a narrow filter bridge of their own, along the tops of other hills down to the tip end opposite Ceylon. A few even jumped the gap, so that the Ceylon hills have a small flora and fauna related in ancestry to the present-day cold-climate creatures of the faraway Himalayas. This is true of the blackbird, certain burrowing snakes, and a host of insects and plants from rhododendrons to barberries and blackberries, suggesting that in an even more tenuous way the mountain species filter from steppingstone to steppingstone just as the lowland species do.

The sequence of invasions of animals by the filter bridge method has happened possibly as many as four times during the million or more years of the Pleistocene epoch. Each of the four ice ages was perhaps correlated in some way with a so-called pluvial, or rainy, period in the tropical latitudes nearer the equator. These climatic shifts allowing the bridge to be established from the mainland over to an adjacent island might have occurred anywhere from 22,000 to 190,000 or more years apart. No one knows how long the bridge might have stayed down and the climate remained the same, but it was at least as long as

10,000 years. Dealing with extended periods like these, it is obvious that an animal species could have undergone considerable evolution during them. Its habits might have changed as pressures of the environment forced it to seek new food sources, or competition with another species might have arisen as a new factor affecting its day-to-day life. In addition, mutations could have changed the genetic constitution of a species in such a time period.

All of this could affect a population isolated from the parent stock. Suppose an animal species managed to reach Ceylon and then gradually became cut off from its Indian relatives. In many millennia the parent species could change remarkably. Suppose then the bridge was restored, making it possible for the parent species once again to cross over?

SOMETHING like this appears to have happened more than once in Ceylon. A small owl, about the size of the American screech owl, is found today in dry deciduous or thorn scrub forest both in south India and Ceylon. It is obviously well adapted to life in these dry places and is not found in rain forests. Instead, there is a Ceylonese rain forest owl almost identical with it except that it has much darker plumage. There is no question that the birds are related. And yet they do not overlap in range, never see one another and hence do not interbreed. How these closely related and yet totally isolated species came into existence is best explained by assuming they are an example of a double invasion via a filter bridge. Assume that back in one of the pluvial periods, when rain forests were widespread, the forest owl was also widespread and managed to work its way through the filter bridge route across India and down into Ceylon. As times changed and the rain forest dwindled, the Ceylon population became isolated. Climatic shifts resulted in a dry-zone environment back in India and the owls there began gradually to adapt themselves to that. When they had a chance to reinvade Ceylon, they not only looked different from their former brothers still living in the rain forest but they preferred a different environment. This effectively kept them apart and ensured that the differences between the two types would be perpetuated if not increased by the passage of time.

The two types of Ceylonese owls still do not meet, but in other cases there may be a mixing of types and a blurring of the picture, with results impossible to forecast. There is a spangled, black, jay-sized bird, widely distributed in India and Ceylon, known as the racket-tailed drongo because its long tail feathers

FROGS AND FILTER BRIDGES

The principle of the filter bridge is well illustrated by frogs in the Philippines. Originally there were no frogs on these islands, but over a period of many million years, as the seas rose and fell, and as land bridges appeared and disappeared, the frogs gradually made their way into the Philippines from Borneo. Today, of Borneo's 89 species, 16 have gotten to Mindanao, 15 to Palawan, and a mere seven to Luzon about 600 miles away. Aquatic frogs had the greatest problem, since they depended on streams and could not easily move overland. By contrast, the terrestrial and arboreal species simply moved through the patches of woodland that grew along these land bridges. The frogs associated with man had the easiest time—many of them were unintentionally carried in boats. Of Luzon's seven species, only one is aquatic, two are terrestrial and arboreal species, and four are associated with man.

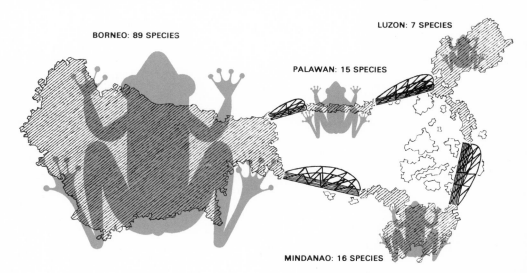

BORNEO: 89 SPECIES

LUZON: 7 SPECIES

PALAWAN: 15 SPECIES

MINDANAO: 16 SPECIES

are shaped like tennis rackets. But in the southwest corner of Ceylon, hidden away in the evergreen rain forest jungle, is a race of drongos that lacks the distinctive tail feathers. Here, obviously, is another example of a double invasion. The interesting thing about this one is that during the last hundred years or so much of the forest between the dry and wet zones has been disturbed by human efforts at farming. Sections of rain forest have been cut and burned, and since this kind of complex vegetation does not regenerate quickly because its characteristic trees need shade in which to grow, other kinds of plants have grown in their place. But the rains continue to fall, and the result is dry-zone forest spreading into wet-zone territory. This is sufficiently confusing to the drongos so that both types enter this "mongrel" jungle, meet each other, breed and produce hybrid offspring. These hybrids resemble their long-tailed, dry-country parents, and for all we know, they may spread into the rain forest and some day replace the ancient, isolated, short-tailed variety and thus destroy another faint bit of evidence of the existence of a filter bridge in the distant past.

T URNING to the second and third types of islands, one will realize immediately that their independent origin and the deep channels that lie between them make any idea of filter bridges impossible. However, they all do contain a profusion of animals and plants, the majority of which are clearly of Asiatic origin. Therefore one must seek another explanation for their populations. The widely accepted one is by the well-known process of island hopping, or, as Simpson calls it, a "sweepstakes route." A sweepstakes route is often exemplified by a continuous chain of islands like steppingstones, with more or less permanent water barriers between. It is up to the animal involved to get across. Some species do, some do not. Ability, luck, viability and long ages of time are involved, since many invasions are accidental and most of these are by single animals and can only end in failure if that animal cannot find a breeding partner. Flying animals obviously can island hop more easily than nonflyers, but even they have their troubles in the tropics, where most flying species are year-round residents and do not quit the area on migratory flights.

A fine example of the sweepstakes principle in operation is seen in the resident bird species of the Lesser Sunda Islands, a group running eastward from Java and Bali. Few better or more obvious sets of steppingstones exist in the world. In Java and Bali there are nearly 200 breeding species of Asiatic birds, but as one goes eastward from island to island, this variety drops drastically. Just east of Bali is the Lombok Strait, a narrow channel only about 30 miles wide, but a deep and ancient one. Across the Strait is the island of Lombok, and of the 200 birds that might have gotten to it across this narrow body of water, 68 have failed to do so. Beyond Lombok is another strait and another island with 10 fewer birds than Lombok. The next island has seven fewer still, the next 24 fewer, and finally at the end of the line the island of Wetar has lost 13 more.

Thus 122 out of 200 Oriental region bird species have been stopped gradually, strait by strait, by these five water gaps. In other animal classes the gaps have been equally effective, and among fresh-water fishes, which in most cases cannot function in salt water at all, the cutoff has been almost complete. Only one species of fresh-water cyprinid fish has got across the Lombok Strait, and the wonder is not so much that only one did, but how that one managed it.

An interesting aspect of this chain of islands is that the farther out toward the end one goes, the nearer one gets to Australia. The easternmost islands in the chain are, in fact, only about 300 miles from the north Australian coast, and there are other islands in between to shorten this long over-water hop. This is quite a flight for nonmigratory birds to make; nevertheless, given storms to blow them and hundreds of thousands or millions of years for the storms to blow, it is probable that some Australian birds should be found in the easternmost islands of the chain. Sure enough, there are some. Not too many, principally because the birds of Australia have gone their own evolutionary way through a tremendously long period of isolation, and as a group are not well equipped to compete with the more varied and more highly developed species of the Asiatic mainland. Nevertheless, certain families have managed to get to the island chain, and a few of these, notably the cockatoos and honey eaters, have made it westward, from island to island, all the way to the Lombok Strait —passing many of the opposite-bound Asiatic birds as they went.

The Lombok Strait, incidentally, is such a clear boundary line separating eastern and western animals that it was used by Wallace as one of the key spots on an imaginary line he drew from south to north in one of the earliest and most original attempts to explain the origin and distribution of species. This is now known as Wallace's Line, and although later investigations have moved the line eastward to make what is known as Weber's Line, the principle still holds good, and the Lombok Strait is still recognized as one of the most ancient and permanent water barriers in that part of the world.

What happens when animals reach an oceanic island and establish themselves? Do they become different, and if so, how? Some interesting insights into this problem are gained by comparing the birds of a large island like Celebes with a very small adjacent one like Unauna. Celebes has a strange swastika shape and consists of four narrow peninsulas all joined together like the legs of a spider without the body. It has its own peculiar animals. Among the mammals there is the highly agile, tree-dwelling, huge-eyed little tarsier. Tarsiers also are found in the Philippine and Sunda island groups, and are of great interest to evolutionists because they are among the more primitive members of a line that is believed to have produced apes and men. The world's ugliest pig, the babirussa, lives on Celebes, as does a bad-tempered, dwarf wild buffalo, the anoa, whose closest known relatives are the tamarau of the Philippines and some fossils from the far-off Himalayas. Certain animals have become extinct on Celebes. One is an elephant—a pygmy about half the size of the elephants of the Asiatic mainland.

T HE birds of Celebes are related to those of neighboring islands—the Philippines to the north, Borneo to the west and Java to the south—and give numerous indications of a long and varied island-hopping relationship with each other and with species on the mainland. All together there are 195 different kinds of birds known to breed on Celebes, a rich but by no means spectacular array. What is interesting is that on the island of Unauna, my own published count made in 1941 shows only 60 species.

If one island can be said to be strongly influenced by another, this could certainly be said of Unauna. A mere dot on the map, only about six and a half miles across, it lies in the center of a huge bay, almost entirely surrounded by two of Celebes' long arms—an island embraced by an island, one might call it. It is volcanic in origin and has a currently active cone. Its underpinning is highly unstable and the island itself is believed to be still rising at a very slow rate. Evidence like this suggests that Unauna's history has been not only short but violent. At most, it may be 15,000 years old. Its volcanic activities, the most

A WELL-TUSKED HOG

The male babirussa of Celebes and Buru Islands has the most elaborate tusks of any hog. The upper tusks of this rare species pierce the roof of the snout and sweep back to the forehead, sometimes measuring 17 inches. Early naturalists believed the curved tusks acted as hooks by which the animal could rest its head on a branch when tired. They are probably just a sexual adornment, however, since those of the females are mere nubs.

recent a mere 65 years ago, have probably made it a rather inhospitable environment during much of that time. Conceivably its 60 bird species have been reduced or wiped out several times in the past and reinforced again from the larger island that surrounds it. A question arises: why have not more of the Celebes birds made their way to Unauna? And another: is 60 the "right" number of species for Unauna to have?

With questions like these we begin to touch some very intricate and interesting problems. To begin with, Unauna could never have as many birds as Celebes, simply because it is much smaller and does not have as many different environments for different kinds of birds to live in. Another inhibitor, however, is not so obvious. That has to do with the fact that birds need territories in which to nest and feed their young. These territories are not normally compressible, and therefore if an island is very small indeed it will be able to support only a very few members of a given species. Very small populations are continually haunted by the specter of extinction, because if old age or accident should afflict the few breeding members of a population, it would then quickly dwindle away to nothing. This is not true of populations of large areas. If a local vacuum is created, it is quickly filled from the surrounding area, but on a small island, there is no surrounding area, and it is reasonable to assume that the animal histories of many little places like Unauna are studded by establishments followed by extinctions and re-establishments followed by re-extinctions. Where the figure of 60 fits on this shifting scale is impossible to say, since it will be determined by the size of the island, the amount of forest, grassland, mangrove swamp and so forth there, by the age of the island and the length of time that has elapsed since the last serious volcanic episode—and finally by the distance to the nearest large land mass. In a general way, what one finds in a place is the right number for that place at that time. And this holds true for a large place like Celebes just as it does for a small one like Unauna.

In the long run, an island fauna will be built up primarily by a series of multiple invasions similar to the example of the owls previously described for Ceylon. These multiple invasions may or may not succeed depending on the "reception committee." An expanding species may arrive in a new habitat to find that its favored mainland environment is already occupied. The new arrival must then adapt to a marginal habitat in order to survive, unless it can outcompete the resident species and take over. Chances are against the latter occurring unless disease or some unfavorable shift in the environment occurs at the same time. E. O. Wilson points out that new arrivals on small archipelagoes or islands often may find vacant niches that were not available to them on the mainland. Here may occur what he calls "ecological release," a rapid expansion into a variety of environments, some of them hitherto closed to it. Great diversification may then result, not only in habits but also in appearance, for evolutionary processes may become speeded up too, and mutations may occur favoring a still wider range of adaptability.

An example of this "ecological release" may be seen on Unauna. An interesting phenomenon of bird populations on islands in the tropics, for instance, is that the bills of island species of birds tend to be larger than those of their relatives on mainlands. The bills do not become larger overnight, of course, but only over thousands of generations. On Unauna I discovered that a species of small dove living on the island had much larger bills than the related population on the mainland of Celebes. Zoologists have noted this phenomenon before

AN ISLAND DWARF

Island mammals are often smaller than their relatives that live on the mainland. This island dwarfism is believed to be an adaptation to the smaller land area available to each animal for feeding and roaming. The domestic water buffalo (upper), common throughout the mainland of tropical Asia, reaches a height of nearly six feet at the shoulder. An island buffalo, the anoa (lower), is the smallest of the world's wild cattle. Found only in the mountains of Celebes, this little animal is slightly more than three feet tall, or half the size of its mainland relative.

in various places, but they have been hard put in the past to account for it.

Recently a possible clue seems to have appeared on the horizon. Janet Kear, an English ornithologist working in Great Britain, noticed that under experimental conditions certain finches chose different seeds to eat than they would have chosen in a state of nature. As these selections were being made, a definite trend occurred toward eating larger seeds. This trend was more marked in certain birds than in others, but the ones that took to it the most wholeheartedly tended to be the ones with the largest bills. In the wild state large seeds are either unobtainable or else they are competed for by other species, so the finches have no opportunity to develop a taste for them, and hence there is no advantage in having a larger bill than normal. But if larger seeds *were* steadily available, it is conceivable that English finches, through adaptation and selection, might have larger bills than they do now. Applying these ideas to Unauna, and visualizing a population of doves free to select among a wide range of seed sizes in its feeding habits because there are no competing doves there, the phenomenon of the large bill begins to seem a little less mysterious. Similarly, a kingfisher on Unauna appears to have a larger bill than its brother on Celebes because it is freed from competition with five other species of Celebes kingfishers. The same thing is true of a starling there.

These few examples do not begin to do justice to the intricate story of speciation and distribution that the island world of Southeast Asia has to tell. But they do illustrate some of the kinds of things one can learn—things that can then be used to formulate principles and be applied to other species and other areas in the gradual unraveling of the story of the continuing development of life. There are doubtless many other lessons to be learned in this unique corner of the world, once the creatures in it have been more thoroughly studied. But the studies must be made quickly, because man is destroying the evidence, both deliberately and accidentally. He is altering environments, wiping out species and introducing others.

A FEW years ago I was sailing north in the Malacca Strait between Malaya and Sumatra in a small freighter and had come on deck to watch the sunrise, an orange to yellow suffusion that lit the oily satin water with an aqueous radiance, turning it from gray to palest bluish-cream. The land-smells from the dozens of nearby islands were all about, a warm earthy smell from the coast south of Padang on the Sumatra side, so flat and low that it lay just "below the wind," as the Malay sailors say. It was then that a tiger, bound from Sumatra for a zoo in Germany, got loose. A Chinese deck hand hosing down the cage below decks let the water play too hard on the beast inside. There was suddenly a lot of noise, a splintering crash, a roaring and the tiger appeared on deck, gave a graceful leap over the rail and plunged into the sea. It evidently smelled the land too, for it swam off at a great rate, straight into the wind, toward the invisible Sumatra coast.

Having breakfast later with the chief engineer we speculated about the tiger. Would he make it?

"Easily," said the engineer. "From here it is about 15 miles to the coast."

It seemed likely. The mouths alone of some of the big rivers of south Sumatra are five miles wide and tigers swim them. Thinking back, it occurred to me that it was lucky that the tiger was a Sumatran tiger and not a Malayan or Indian animal. So long as it was swimming to Sumatra it might as well belong to that population and not start any double invasions elsewhere.

SPRAWLED ON A JUNGLE ROCK, A YOUNG ORANG SHOWS THE ENGAGING GRIN AND PLAYFUL MANNER THAT MAKE HIM SO DESIRED AS A PET

The Island Sanctuaries

Islands are the closest things to living laboratories found in the natural world. Isolated by the sea, their flora and fauna may profit from lack of competition or exploit local opportunities to take on new forms. Offshore islands may be refuges for species which have died out on the mainland, like the orangutan; remoter oceanic islands may foster giants, like the largest living lizards on earth.

ONE WHO SURVIVED, A YOUNG ORANG RESCUED FROM CAPTIVITY FROLICS IN A JUNGLE ENCLOSURE IN BAKO NATIONAL PARK IN SARAWAK.

The Long Road toward Extinction

Less than half a million years ago, when man was starting his rise to dominance in the animal world, orangutans roamed throughout Southeast Asia and its islands. Large and powerful, these Oriental representatives of the great apes had few natural enemies and a plentiful supply of food available in the fruits, green leaves and tender young branches which they plucked in the canopy of the rain forest trees. Orangutans are highly intelligent apes. They are amiable and curious too, and these qualities, plus their strikingly human appearance, have always made them peculiarly fascinating to man. Although they were hunted by Stone Age man, and perhaps even kept as pets in Stone Age caves,

NAMED ARTHUR BY ITS FOSTER MOTHER, BARBARA HARRISSON, IT IS BEING USED IN A UNIQUE EFFORT TO REINTRODUCE ORANGS TO THE WILD

changes in climate were probably the principal factors in reducing their numbers. In any event, it is fairly certain that by Neolithic times they existed only in two widely separated areas on Sumatra and Borneo. There, with the coming of the Europeans in the 17th Century, they were subjected to terrible slaughter; what with being killed as scientific specimens and captured for zoos, their numbers shrank, until today only about 2,500 individuals survive. In a desperate effort to save them from certain extinction, Mrs. Barbara Harrisson, wife of the curator of the Sarawak Museum, is attempting to train young orangs, intercepted in the black-market zoo trade, to relearn the ways of living in the wild.

IN THE WILD, the young orang Arthur munches a pandanus fruit. Now age five and introduced to jungle life, he builds the orang's typical nests of branches and twigs, and subsists almost entirely on his own. But in all this, he had to be guided: orangs reared in captivity must literally be educated to live away from the humans who have taken care of them.

IN CAPTIVITY, the orang Andy of New York's Bronx Zoo has grown enormously fat and lethargic—conditions uncharacteristic of orangs in the wild. Cheek and throat pouches are huge exaggerations of normal growths in adult males, but the lump on his head appears to be pure fat. Once playful and curious, Andy now weighs over 400 pounds and rarely moves.

TUMBLING ABOUT ON THE FOREST FLOOR, BIG ARTHUR AND LITTLE CYNTHIA PLAY AND WRESTLE IN THE MANNER TYPICAL OF SUBADULT ORANGS

The Way Back to the Wild

When Arthur came to live with Mrs. Harrisson, he was about two and a half years old. With him came a female named Cynthia, 18 months old. These two were to be the principal protagonists in the drama of training orangs back to a wild life—a process that would take years.

The first step, to accustom the young apes to live outside their cages, was accomplished in the garden of the Harrisson house in Kuching. After six months, both were deemed ready for the next stage: a semiwild life in a 20-by-40-foot wire-mesh enclosure erected in virgin rain forest in Bako National Park. There, after initial great excitement, both developed distinctly different attitudes toward their new world. Arthur's interests focused on the jungle outside, but Cynthia clung to the safety of the enclosure. After two months, Arthur would go off on his own for several hours at a time, but Cynthia had to be carried out and guided to familiarity with the forest. Three years after the experiment began, the two orangs were still not entirely on their own, but it was clear that in time they could be and, with others trained to wilderness life in the same way, might perpetuate their species.

BACK WITH MOTHER, Arthur joins Mrs. Harrisson in a frolic on the beach near the feeding station which marks his last link with man. Attendants still supplement his food every day.

114

WALKING LIKE A MAN, Arthur flings his arms high for balance, imitating *Homo sapiens*. On the ground, his usual form of locomotion is a rolling, sideways gait on all fours or an exuberant head over heels tumble. This beach is visited occasionally by both Arthur and Cynthia, who play with crabs and pebbles there, but they have never been seen entering the water.

115

A SHORT-TAILED DRONGO lacks the head plumes of its cousins and has a deeply forked tail. One of some 20 species, this bird closely resembles the Ceylonese form, which is quite rare.

The Quirks of Isolation

Animals, like humans, develop special characteristics if they are isolated long enough on islands. Sometimes this is simply because the lack of other competitive animals gives them broader opportunities: a seed-eating bird may branch out and evolve subspecies that feed on insects, nectar or even fish. Sometimes a change in climate may result in the evolution of a new type, as in the case of a jay-sized, blue-black bird, a species of drongo (above), found exclusively in a wet, mountain evergreen forest in Ceylon. The difference between this drongo and its close relatives (left), which live in other parts of Ceylon, is that—isolated by climatic changes—it has lost the long, racket-shaped tail and head crest characteristic of the species.

Sometimes islands even foster such curious developments as the long and flexible nose of the male proboscis monkey—an appendage which seems to have no relationship to what this animal eats or does, and is even inexplicable in terms of its relatives, the closest of which, in this case, probably live in China and have more normal noses. And tropical Asia, as the following pages show, has one animal which in isolation has turned into a giant—either from lack of any competition by other predators or perhaps because of a mutation of its genes which was perpetuated, unchecked, through the ages.

A LONG-TAILED DRONGO guards two young in its cradlelike nest. Large and aggressive, these drongos often attack bigger birds; this one has lost one tail feather, probably in a fight.

ANOTHER ISLANDER, a proboscis monkey of Borneo, rests in a boat after being picked up at sea. Only male adults develop long noses—a quirk perhaps due to a preference of the females.

A Legend Come to Life

Black and bony of hide, with a long, double-forked, yellow tongue that flicks in and out like a flame, the Komodo "dragon" of the Lesser Sundas seems the progenitor of all the fire-breathing dragons known in legends. Its size is awe-inspiring: this largest of all lizards reaches 12 feet in length and a weight of 300 pounds. Where it came from nobody knows; it lives today on only three small islands, where its species thrived undiscovered by man until a bare half-century ago. Volcanic in origin, this group emerged in the beginning of the Pleistocene, and it is possible that the dragons' ancestors swam there from adjoining islands and then, kings of their tiny and isolated realms, developed their giant forms.

ON THE ALERT, a Komodo "dragon" tests the air with flicking tongue. Though they eat carrion, they also run down such fast animals as goats, deer and wild boar.

ON THE BEACH, the giant lizard walks in lonely dignity: no other predator here reaches this size. Komodos shelter at night in burrows, where they may sleep for days.

6

An Insect
Treasure Trove

Nowhere in the world, with the possible exception of South America, are insects more staggeringly abundant, varied and specialized than in Southeast Asia. Here the entomologist faces an almost hopeless task. Some experts say flatly that there are so many thousands of insects in the area awaiting discovery that the task of collecting and classifying them may never be complete. The experience of the Oxford University Expedition to Sarawak in 1932 gives some idea of the wealth of the insect fauna. Two undergraduate entomologists working in the field for six months made such extensive collections that the scientific papers describing only the new species they found form an enormous volume. More than 30 years later, entomologists are still working on these collections, identifying new forms.

Why should there be so many insects in Southeast Asia? For one thing, this region has long served as a center of evolution from which many types have spread out to other areas. On the other hand, it also lies fairly close to two other continents with entirely different faunas—Australia and Africa—and has received and still receives new forms from them. Still another factor is the island nature of so much of Southeast Asia, which has given many kinds of insects

THE DUNG SPIDER

One of the most unusual camouflages in the entire animal world is that displayed by a small spider from Ceylon and Java. It spins an irregular white web on a leaf, then stations itself in the middle —the whole thing, web and spider, looking exactly like the chalky-white splash of a bird-dropping with a dark, dried center. This serves a double function; not only does it permit the spider to grab butterflies that come to feed on the supposed bit of excrement but it also helps conceal the spider from marauding wasps.

the rare opportunity to evolve in relative isolation and to speciate widely. But the most important reason by far is the rain forest. Here are found all the conditions that suit insects best. Not only is there a wide range of niches for them to occupy, from the ground itself to the top of the canopy, but there is a limitless supply of food of all kinds in the many thousands of different species of trees, to say nothing of the smaller plants. And each tree can support a host of specialized insects, some feeding only on buds, others only on leaves, still others only on flowers, young bark or wood. In addition, the lack of regular seasons and the over-all warmth and high humidity are conducive to reproduction, food gathering and other activities throughout the year, and as a result, insects need not hibernate or estivate to avoid the rigors of winter or the hazards of a dry summer.

IT is easy to show what an evolutionary impact the rain forest has had on the insects of Southeast Asia by citing just one group, the Orthoptera—the walking sticks, katydids, mantids, cockroaches, crickets and grasshoppers. Take the matter of size, for example. There are walking sticks over seven inches long, crickets so small they resemble minute shreds of bark, and katydids that grow to the length of a man's hand. But it is in camouflage that the Orthoptera excel. In addition to looking like sticks and twigs, walking sticks in the rain forests of Borneo have come to resemble scraps of vines. Others have developed irregular flanges of dark green, brown and gray on their legs, which make them highly conspicuous as they move about but help to disguise them when they stand still. Stop one in its tracks and it will stretch out its front and hind legs —and suddenly look like a dead twig covered with lichens. Walking sticks even carry their plant disguises down to their eggs, which resemble seeds and are strewn on the ground by the female while she is feeding. Some species that do not mimic sticks, twigs or other vegetable matter are covered with long, hard, unbelievably sharp spines. The only way to collect them is to wrap a leaf around them or wear leather gloves. They are usually ignored by birds and mammals but have been found inside the stomachs of monitor lizards, which goes to prove that no protective device is perfect.

Among the masters of disguise of the Orthoptera are the mantids. Some are merely green, which helps to conceal them in foliage as they lie in wait for their prey. But some are also flat and have veins, bruise spots and other blemishes that make them look almost exactly like flowers. One even mimics a dead leaf. *Hymenopus coronatus* starts out life a bright red with black spots and bears such a close resemblance to the young of an unpalatable plant bug that it is bypassed by many predators. After the next molt, it becomes—and remains to the end of its life—flowerlike. In its larval stage it is generally a bright pink with a green bar on the prothorax. Sitting motionless on a branch, it keeps the rear end of its body arched over its back and flares out petal-like extensions of its legs. People have been known to examine it without realizing that it was an animal. Upon becoming adult, it turns cream-colored. Obviously such mimicry helps protect the mantid but may have another advantage as well. Resembling a flower, it attracts insects in search of nectar—insects on which the mantid then can feed.

A favorite food of some mantids is their relatives, the cockroaches, which abound throughout Southeast Asia and show curious habits and adaptations. Although some live in human dwellings, the majority live in the forests, in decaying wood, in flowers, under stones or dead leaves, on tree trunks and even in and around water. A few are brilliantly colored, quite unlike the household variety; others are streaked and mottled, and difficult to spot on trees. Several so approximate plant-feeding beetles and ladybirds that entomologists are hard put to identify them properly.

With opportunities for specialization in Southeast Asia so enormously varied, the insects have undoubtedly come to play assorted roles in the ecology of the forest. But precisely what these are no one can say, so unstudied is the region as a whole. About all that can be said with certainty is that insects contribute enormously to the success of most of the vertebrates by providing them directly or indirectly with food, and to the success of the forest by clearing away litter and converting it to soil. When a tree dies, it draws beetles from all around whose larvae bore into the wood even while the tree is still standing. Their tunnels admit moisture, and the dampness in turn encourages the growth of parasitic fungi. Termites or ants soon colonize the rotting wood, which becomes more and more friable until in the end the trunk is nothing more than a cylinder of rich humus—by which time, of course, it has long since fallen to the forest floor.

Ants, termites and Collembola, mostly small and unrelated creatures, seem to make the biggest contribution to the cycle of life in the tropics. Most termites subsist solely on dead wood. But, as essential as they are to the ecology of the forest, they can also be pests, chewing through timbers and stored books or, as in the case of species that eat living wood, attacking valuable stands of rubber trees. One species that lives underground even destroys the lead casing around electric cables, causing power failures. It does so not because it has an appetite for lead but simply because the cables sometimes block the advance of its tunnels. Several termites raise fungi on decaying vegetable matter. The commonest Malaysian species, *Macrotermes*, grows fungi right inside its moundlike nest. Another closely related species forages at night for detritus with which to fertilize its fungus gardens.

THE SEXTON BEETLE

A husky one-and-a-half-inch insect, this beetle is attracted to small corpses by the smell of their decaying flesh. A few beetles, gathering around and under a dead mouse, will begin digging away the earth beneath it, and within two or three hours will have completely buried it. If the ground is hard, they sometimes drag it several feet to a spot where digging is easier. Speed is important, for they must get the corpse buried and their eggs laid in its flesh before it is infested with the maggots of carrion flies.

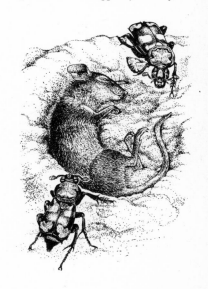

T ERMITES, although not always seen, are conspicuous in the forest setting because of the nests they build. Some construct globular nests, covered with a blackish crust, high among the branches of trees. Others erect curiously shaped pillars of earth on the ground. Life within these dwellings is fascinating to observe. The king termite, the consort who fertilizes the queen, starts with wings but soon sheds them, retaining only stumps. The queen, after fertilization, undergoes a marvelous change, growing enormously after her last molt, the only insect to do so. The abdomen enlarges to a sausage-shaped structure from which may come more than 40,000 eggs in 24 hours—and millions over a lifetime. Worker termites build and maintain the nest, and soldiers defend it. Soldiers of the genus *Nasutitermes* have a tapering snout out of which they can eject a sticky fluid that will gum up and immobilize an ant, the termites' implacable enemy.

Ants are literally all over the place in the forest, including the top of the canopy. Many have taken to living inside plants—in the leaves, fronds, stems, tubers and roots. This is apparently most often a one-sided relationship, although a few may pay for their keep by driving off insects that might eat the plant hosts.

The ants, along with some beetles, especially scarabs, and some other insects, such as flies, dispose of the great bulk of dead animals in the forest. Throughout much of Southeast Asia there is a dearth of vultures and other big

123

AN AIRBORNE ANT HOME

A common epiphyte in Malaysia is Myr-mecodia, which grows on mangroves and in turn provides a home for ants. The bulk of this air plant is a large tuber-like structure. When the plant is young this is solid, but as it grows older it dries out, becomes corky and riddled with air spaces (below). It is then that the ants move in, finding a snug home ready-made. The plant probably gets nothing in return, although it may derive some slight nourishment from ant excrement or protection against leaf-eaters, which the ants might drive away. But these are fringe benefits, since many myrmecodias thrive without any ant tenants at all.

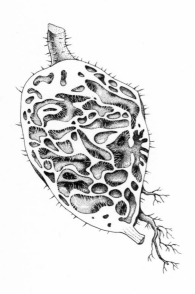

carrion eaters. In the rain forest, the cover is so dense and so many different odors fill the air that the news of carrion does not carry far by either sight or smell. There are no birds that are carrion eaters at all, and only a few mammals that do so, while among the reptiles only monitor lizards eat carrion (though this is not their main source of food). Thanks largely to the insects, however, decay is extremely rapid. Within minutes, ants and others begin to dispose of dead—and even dying—animals of all kinds and sizes, from fleas to elephants.

The ants come in amazing varieties as well as numbers. A common species that gets into every home in Southeast Asia is Pharaoh's ant, only a twelfth of an inch long, yellow with a dark tip to its tail. Like the Norwegian rat and the American cockroach, it has been carried all over the world in ships. Though a tropical ant, it quickly adjusts itself and is becoming established in heated buildings in many cool countries. But the ant most likely to be noticed is the giant ant *(Camponotus gigas)*, which is an inch long and dull brown. It usually wanders about on the forest floor and along any path, solitary or in small groups. It can give a good nip but is by nature unaggressive, unlike the Keringa ant, which is much smaller and lives in colonies inside clusters of leaves woven together with silk. A man can brush against a Keringa colony easily enough, but it will not be easy for him to forget the discourtesy. Not only is the bite painful but each pair of jaws ejects a fluid that burns on the tiny wound.

In the bushy plants just back of a mangrove swamp in Java, I once had my first encounter with Keringa ants and watched them making a nest. They are red, long-legged and about half an inch long. The nest is made by joining leaves together; this one was as big as a football. A falling branch had torn a hole in it, and ants were swarming all over the open tear. I watched a company of workers hold a fresh leaf over the gap while other workers held a number of small, squirming creatures, the larvae of the ants themselves, carried out of the interior of the nest to make repairs. For these helpless larvae are capable of spinning silk, even though they do not make cocoons, and it is their silk which holds the nest together. As the worker ants passed the larvae back and forth over the appressed edges of the new and old leaves, they looked like weavers holding the shuttles of an old-fashioned loom. Out of the silk glands of the larvae each worker squeezed a whitish stream, forming a thread of glue which, drying in the air, made a solid web of great strength. And so the nest was re-paired.

THERE are also ants that sting instead of bite. One to avoid in this category is *Tetraponera*, the fire ant. It is reddish, rather long in the body and has a black tailtip. Though fire ants nest inside hollow branches, they come out forag-ing in the best-kept gardens, and to stumble among them is another of life's unforgettable experiences.

Finally, there are the so-to-speak underprivileged ants, the ponerines. Shin-ing black, they live in small groups under fallen logs and lack the well-organized nests and elaborate social organization of the other ants. They can give a really nasty sting.

From the point of view of the traveler, however casual, the butterflies and the moths, the dragonflies and the beetles, rather than the ants or termites, are the insects most often seen in Southeast Asia, while the cicadas, followed by the grasshoppers and crickets, are the ones most often—and often continuously—heard. Moths are even more numerous than the butterflies. One of the most extraordinary, as well as the biggest, is Atlas, whose wings, patterned in shades of rich brown with a transparent "window" in each, are 10 inches across; even its pale green caterpillars grow to a length of four and a half inches. Perhaps the most powerful fliers, however, are the narrow-winged, stout-bodied hawk moths. The smooth, hairless larva of one of these bears a conspicuous eyespot which it can manipulate in such a fashion that it looks strikingly like the head of a snake. Yet another group with remarkable larvae are the bagworm moths. From tiny twigs and scraps of vegetation or other materials, the caterpillars fashion silk-lined cases, each species following its own pattern. The larvae remain in the cases, dragging them about like shells, and later pupate in them. Only the males grow wings; the females lay their eggs and die in the cases they occupied as larvae. Powerful and speedy fliers, dragonflies glisten and sparkle in the sunshine as they dart about. They too are found almost everywhere but are never more numerous and varied than around water, in which they pass the early stages of their lives. A close relative is the small black-bodied damsel fly, with dark, transparent wings with iridescent blue upper surfaces. When this insect is at rest, with its wings pressed together above its body, it is all but invisible, but in flight it seems to flash on and off, like a tiny, blue, electric light, as its wings move up and down in the sunshine.

BEETLES fly about nearly as much as butterflies and dragonflies but seem to get into one's life considerably more. They pop up everywhere, from the top of the canopy down to the humus of the forest floor. The smallest are almost microscopic, the largest fill the palm of the hand.

Wallace was amazed by their numbers. Studying the insect fauna of the island of Singapore in 1854, he wrote, "In about two months I obtained no less than 700 species of beetles, a large proportion of which were quite new, and among them were 130 different kinds of the elegant Longicorns (*Cerambycidae*), so much esteemed by collectors. Almost all these were collected in one patch of jungle not more than a mile square in extent."

Wallace's classic enterprise with beetles, however, was carried out near the coal mines on the Sadong River in west Borneo one year later. Not only is it one of the most extensive collections of the kind ever made but it also represents the first attempt to make a systematic collection of any exact group within any one locality and habitat, again nearly all within a square mile of ground. Now, more than a century later, we know very little more about the ecology of beetles or any other insects—and nothing about a total ecology of all the animals within one square mile (or one square yard) of Southeast Asian rain forest, though the knowledge would be a fundamental contribution to our understanding of the whole area. Wallace wrote of his Bornean beetle collecting:

"When I arrived at the mines, on the 14th of March, I had collected in the four preceding months 320 different kinds of beetles. In less than a fortnight I had doubled this number, an average of about 24 new species every day. On one day I collected 76 different kinds, of which 34 were new to me. By the end of April I had more than a thousand species, and they went on increasing at a slower rate; so that I obtained altogether in Borneo about two thousand distinct kinds, of which all but about a hundred were collected at this place, and on scarcely more than a square mile of ground. The most numerous and most interesting groups of beetles were the Longicorns and Rhynchophora, both preeminently wood-feeders. The former, characterized by their graceful forms and long antennae, were especially numerous, amounting to nearly three hundred species, nine-tenths of which were entirely new, and many of them remarkable

WASPS IN THE LEAVES

Trees supply many of tropical Asia's solitary wasps with nest-building materials. Zethus (above) makes use of the leathery leaves of the bancal tree, chewing them into small pieces and then gluing them together with its own saliva. This is a long process and takes the hard-working female several months to complete. Stenogaster (below) chews decayed wood from fallen trees into a pulp, masticating it into a crude paper, and from this constructs a nest on a stem or under an overhanging bank or rock. On the stem above the nest is sometimes put an "ant guard," a small ring of the same pulpy stuff to keep ants out of the nest.

for their large size, strange forms, and beautiful colouring. The latter correspond to our weevils and allied groups, and in the tropics are exceedingly numerous and varied, often swarming upon dead timber, so that I sometimes obtained fifty or sixty different kinds in a day."

The Italian naturalist Dr. Odoardo Beccari, in the same part of Borneo 20 years later, had another experience with beetles which beautifully illustrates the richness of the insect fauna and the discomforts attendant upon the naturalist at work in the tropics:

"This same day, before sunrise," Beccari wrote, "I made an extraordinary haul of very small insects, mostly micro-*Coleoptera*. The torrential rain of the previous day had evidently been a veritable Flood for a whole world of small creatures which the violence of the water had washed off the plants, forcing them to seek safety on every floating fragment. And now the waters of the stream retiring had left high and dry on the banks all this flotsam and jetsam covered with myriads of ship-wrecked creatures, which it was easy work to capture. Some of these extempory rafts, I found, were loaded with heads, abdomens, legs and other fragments of insects which had been destroyed by the flood. These *Coleoptera* were all the more easy to catch owing to their being half drowned or reduced to a condition of torpor owing to the cold of the previous nights. I might have gone on catching them had it not been for the mosquitoes and sandflies, but these came out in myriads and tormented me so incessantly that I eventually had to bring to a conclusion what had been a most successful morning's hunt."

The largest of the beetles is the scarab. One of these, the two-inch-long rhinoceros beetle, attacks coconut palms and is considered a pest by man. Among the most beautiful of the beetles are the metallic wood borers, whose gaudiest member, the gold-green jewel beetle, is used as a setting for jewelry and often even thrust entirely through the ear lobe as an ornament by tribal people in the hills.

Among the conspicuous Coleoptera are the long-horned beetles, which have antennae that in repose sweep back round the body and past the hind legs. Certainly one of the commonest is *Batocera*, a long-horned beetle. One species has brilliant yellow spots on its gray upper wings, and red marks on its curiously spined body. If touched, it produces a clicking noise by moving its thorax.

O NE of the oddest looking is the tortoise beetle (Cassidinae), which because of its size seems more like a miniature tortoise than a medium-sized beetle. It is part of a larger group, the so-called leaf beetles, many of which may be seen basking in the sun on the leaves of bushes and big trees. The tortoise beetles have their elytra—the hard, metallic wing cases—expanded into semicircular shields with another shield arcing out round the front of the head, so that only two small antennae and the two front legs project when the insects are at rest. They come in brilliant colors; perhaps the brightest is yellow, spotted with black or gold. But unlike the jewel beetles their lovely colors quickly fade in death.

Many beetles come out only at night. A camp in the forest, or even a house in a rubber plantation, will have its lights bombarded by beetles of many kinds. Some are sure to be skipjacks or click beetles (Elateridae) which, upon hitting a bulb, fall to the floor and remain dead still, even if upside down. But they are shamming death; in a moment they release a kind of mousetrap mechanism which throws them into the air with a click and eventually lands them right side up again.

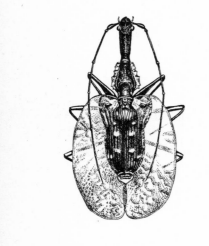

THE FIDDLE BEETLE

This is one of four species of odd violin-shaped beetles found in Borneo, Java and Sumatra, and once believed so rare that a French museum paid nearly $200 for a specimen. Actually, they are fairly common, though not frequently seen, for despite their large size (about four inches) they are extremely flat and can hide in small crevices under bark. There they find the grubs and eggs of other insects, their long, flat heads making it easier for them to probe deep for food.

Less conspicuous but almost as ubiquitous as the beetles are the cicadas, katydids and crickets—the prime noisemakers of the forest. The most clamorous of these are the cicadas. Each species calls in its own special way and usually announces itself at a particular time of day. The cicadas sound off so punctually that it is possible to tell time by them. One species about the size of a sparrow sets up a deafening din at 6 p.m., plus or minus 15 minutes, and has been dubbed the Dayak clock by entomologists familiar with its call. Its timetable is thrown off only when the sky has been overcast all day.

Mosquitoes, like the cicadas and beetles, are also very common, as might be expected, in swampy areas. Flies, on the other hand, are less common in the forest—their habitat is open country or towns, where sanitation is poor. The biting sandflies of the seashore, riverbanks, mangroves and inland scrub jungle can be pests of the worst sort. They are so small that they pass right through mosquito netting. For a long time it was thought that sandflies carried dengue fever and other diseases, but a recent great acceleration in research has shown that many more kinds of mosquito exist than had previously been thought and that they are responsible for the supposed sins of the sandflies.

MALARIA is, of course, the most common disease carried by certain species of mosquito of the genus *Anopheles*, all of which identify themselves by the way they cock their tails up when not in flight. This had been known for many years, but continuing research has shown that quite a few anopheline species are malaria carriers and that they live in different habitats and perhaps transmit different forms of malaria. Thus, for instance, one species is commonly the carrier in hill country, another on the coastal plains, and a third along the coast where it lives in brackish water.

Modern science can count as one of its truly great successes the eradication of malaria from vast areas of Southeast Asia through spraying carried out by the World Health Organization. The effects have been immediate and sensational —for instance, a very big drop in infant mortality. Unfortunately, some mosquito strains are now acquiring resistance to insecticides, while the insecticides themselves have produced acute side problems. One of the oddest problems to date resulted when spraying also killed off the cockroaches living in the Dayak long houses of Borneo. These cockroaches were one of the principal foods of Borneo house cats, and when the cats had a feast of poisoned cockroaches, they died off too, and whole native tribes became catless overnight. The rats and mice overran the long houses and eventually became so numerous and fierce that rats began chewing the toes of children.

Another side effect showed a little more slowly. It had not been realized that the cockroaches, though a nuisance in the long houses, had been serving the invaluable subsidiary purpose of eating bed bugs once these got beyond a certain size. A few months after the cat crisis came a bedbug crisis—the long houses for the first time began to crawl with them. Now there is a demand for vigorous cockroaches in Borneo's interior.

Bees and hornets are numerous in Southeast Asia; several species of bees, in fact, have been domesticated by man in a variety of ways. In parts of Java and the southern Philippines, wild bees are persuaded to swarm in specially constructed wooden drums under the eaves of the houses. The bee of the Koompassia tree, the "honey tree" of the rain forest, is *Megapis dorsata*, common as far west as Pakistan. By sophisticated standards, its honey would be regarded as of poor quality, but in most Asian diets there is a shortage of sugar, and some of the tribes, in places where sugar cane grows poorly, have a passion for honey which will take them to any heights.

Curiously enough, certain species of bees in Southeast Asia make honey which seems to be poisonous. There is as yet no scientific proof for this, but several well-authenticated cases have been reported of people dying after eating honey of the wrong kind. According to the natives, the culprits are bees that live inside dead trees and bamboos, with the main axis of the nest parallel to the ground, i.e., not up and down.

Some Southeast Asian bees are feared for their stings, but they certainly are less feared than the hornets. One hornet is rated among the top most dangerous animals of Southeast Asia by many of the jungle peoples—along with the tiger and wild buffalo, the honey bear (when it has young), the hamadryad, or king cobra, the crocodile and the sea snake. This is *Vespa tropica*, the banded hornet, with a wing span of about four inches. Because it has a bright orange stripe across its black abdomen, it is called the tiger hornet in many different languages of the area.

Tiger hornets commonly nest low down in hollow trees or rotten roots, sometimes in holes under the leaves. The colonies are small and move from one place to another. Danger arises when a colony suddenly settles beside a well-used jungle track or plantation path, and the first person coming along accidentally stirs up the hornets. One or two stings can be endured, but if the whole gang attacks, the result can be fatal, even for strong men in good health.

THE habits of this hornet explain a feature of jungle life which greatly annoys the logical Westerner. He often finds it an inexplicable nuisance that tracks wind about all over the place, instead of going straight on through what looks like perfectly easy, flat country. One naturalist, in the days of his inexperience, insisted on having a straight track made for about four miles through a jungle area which he was constantly crossing during the course of a continuous nature-study project. The natives, polite as ever, obliged. He could see they thought he was crazy, but then *he* thought they were crazy not to like it that way when it was to their own advantage. He did not go back to this particular place for another six years—when he discovered that the track was again as crooked as ever. He also discovered that in those intervening years, enough hornets had built their nests alongside the trail to make wide, looping detours around them extremely expedient. For it is much easier to avoid the nests than try to get them out.

Outstanding among the many different kinds of wasps inhabiting the region are solitary wasps, which as adults feed on nectar and other insects, often showing a preference for one species, genus or family over another, or even for one sex. They sting their prey into paralysis and devour it entirely or in part; sometimes they will chew its neck and lap up the juices that ooze forth. Solitary wasps represent one of the few types of insects to make provision for their young after they hatch. The female occasionally enters houses and makes its nest of mud pellets in everything from a keyhole to the fold of a curtain, where it can be watched laying in a supply of food, generally spiders or caterpillars, which are sealed away with the eggs. The victims of course are not dead but merely paralyzed, and do not decompose during the incubation period. "Guided by an instinct as infallible as that which instructed its mother," writes one observer, "the tiny maggot which is to become a wasp starts its meal with care to avoid its victim's vital organs, and thus preserves it alive until the last possible moment."

THE BRIGHT METALLIC COLOR OF A LEAF BEETLE GLEAMS AGAINST A YELLOW BLOSSOM. ON SHADED LEAVES, IT WOULD BE ALMOST INVISIBLE

An Insect Melting Pot

Insects, ruggedly built, prolific and often endowed with flight, make good colonizers of new environments. Southeast Asia offers them many opportunities: a tropical climate, a rich vegetation and a location at the crossroads between Africa, Australia and the great Asian land mass. Consequently, there are more diverse species here per square mile than in any other area of the world.

129

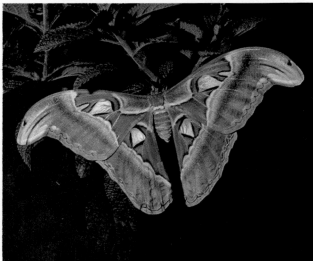

THE ATLAS MOTHS of tropical Asia, two of which are shown above, have the largest wing area of any Lepidoptera, though their span is exceeded by one of the South American moths.

Large Lepidoptera

The very sprawl of tropical Asia often allows for wide variation within a single genus of animals. This is particularly noticeable among the large Lepidoptera, such as the atlas moths above—the upper one comes from India and the lower one from Malaya. Another variation in form is seasonal rather than regional. Places like India are likely to produce a phenomenon called seasonal dimorphism—the development of two forms because of marked wet and dry periods. During the rainy season certain butterflies are distinctly larger, brighter and more numerous than their dry-season brothers.

RAJA BROOKE'S BIRDWING, named to honor the British soldier who once ruled Sarawak, is among the largest and most beautiful of butterflies. Here, as is their habit, males have

gathered to drink at a forest seepage. Females, paler and with white spots on their wings, remain in the upper stories of the forest. Because they are so seldom seen, it was long sup-

posed that male birdwings outnumbered females by 1,000 to 1, a discrepancy which seemed quite inexplicable since these are mating insects. The ratio is now considered about equal.

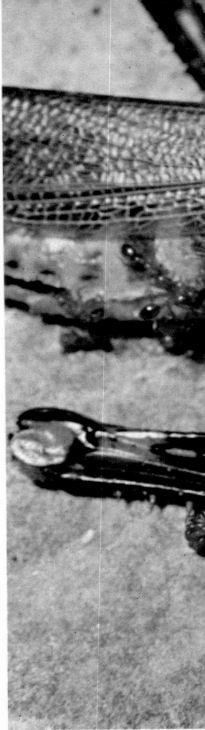

DISMEMBERING THE CORPSE, a colony of scavenging ants will strip this short-horned locust of all its edible parts in a few minutes. Thus are the dead of the forest disposed of almost as quickly as they fall.

THE LIVE BODY of a walking stick apparently can fool even an ant. Marching blithely down the insect's upraised foreleg toward its head, the ant is in no danger, since stick insects are strict vegetarians.

Rain Forest Garbagemen

The locust in the picture above was laid low by parasitic mites or some similar affliction, but now that it is dead it is the turn of the ants to feast upon it. When one of these tiny but efficient forest scavengers makes such a rich discovery, it is only a matter of minutes before other members join it on the carcass, arriving in answer to the worker's signal. Excited by finding food, a worker ant stridulates, a process similar to that of a locust rubbing its spurred legs against its wings. In the ant, stridulation is produced by rapidly rubbing together two abdominal segments, one notched, the other pointed, making a noise that other ants can hear but which is too high-pitched for the human ear.

A FLOWER MANTID mimics the orchid on which it sits so closely that it is hard to tell where one begins and the other leaves off. The insect's expanded thighs resemble the petals of the flower, its delicately striped hind part the flower's center. Sitting motionless among the blossoms, it is hidden from predators, waiting, itself a predator, to seize whatever small, unsuspecting insects may come here to feed.

135

A POTTER WASP stuffs a paralyzed caterpillar into a mud chamber to feed the egg it has deposited inside. This solitary species is lower on the evolutionary ladder than social wasps.

The Resourceful Wasps

Tropical wasps recognize no season; they mature, build after their fashion, procreate and die in an endless, repetitious cycle without pause. Beyond that, the difference between them and the wasps of the temperate climate is merely a matter of detail —but often the detail is fascinating. *Stenogaster*, for example (*right*), which is at home in the forest shadows from Australia north to the Philippines, puts its vulnerable larvae for protection in a pencil-thin nest hung by a long thread. But even this would not effectively deter the ants, which climb everywhere, so *Stenogaster* produces an "ant guard"— a sticky, repellent substance with which it coats a portion of the thread by which the nest is hung. Despite this care, the nest is still frequently ravaged and the larvae carried off by another, more aggressive wasp, *Vespa deusta*, which finds *Stenogaster* a perfect source of food needed by its own larvae.

SUSPENDED FOR SAFETY, the slim nest of a *Stenogaster* wasp has chambers opening on a central shaft through which a half dozen males and females tend the larvae.

FOUNDING A COLONY, a paper wasp begins a nest that will eventually look like a plate. A daughter will soon appear out of the capped chamber to help the mother.

An Extraordinary Weaver

The huge spider below, seven inches across, which sucks the life from its insect victims, is in turn eaten with gusto by the Lao people of northern Thailand —either raw or lightly toasted and dipped in salt. To get the insects it requires for food, this *Nephila* spider has developed weaving to an extraordinary art. Small birds occasionally get entangled in its huge web, which is sometimes eight feet wide and is made from golden silk stronger and more beautiful than that of the silkworm. Because of its excellent quali-ties, various attempts have been made over the years to harvest *Nephila* silk commercially, but the problems involved are formidable. A spider web cannot be unraveled the way a silkworm cocoon can. The only way to obtain a usable thread is to draw the silk from the live animal—a process which involves strapping down a large number of the spiders and slowly drawing silk filaments out of each, at the same time twisting them together to form a thread of suitable thickness that is then wound on a reel.

MAKING A CATCH, a female silk spider seizes a mantid. On her back, out of reach, rides her tiny consort, who thus avoids the danger of being eaten himself by his enormous mate.

WARDING OFF PREDATORS, a little spiny-bodied spider from Malaya brandishes backward-pointing horns—extreme developments of the spines which give this subfamily its name.

Wallace's Delight: the Long-horned Beetles

Beetles were collected by Alfred Russel Wallace in greater numbers than any other form of animal life during his six-year stay in the Malay Archipelago more than a hundred years ago. Of all, the most interesting to him were the enormously abundant and diverse Cerambycidae, the longicorns or long-horned beetles. He looked for them everywhere he went, and nearly every one he found was new to science. The 15 longicorns above, shown nearly life size, represent but a tiny fraction of the more than 20,000 species known worldwide today. Wallace himself collected more than 1,000 species; many hundreds have been discovered since, and hundreds more, certainly, still await discovery. The largest of those shown here *(upper right)* was found on the Malay Peninsula and grows four inches or more in

length; the smallest *(lower left)*, just under an inch, comes from Borneo. In the family as a whole the longicorns show an even greater size range, from less than a quarter inch to at least six inches. The prominent antennae are usually longer in the male than in the female and may be three times as long as the body—in extreme cases, even five times as long. Like most insect antennae, they serve as smell receptors—

the male uses this extra-long "nose" at mating time, to pick up the female's scent.

The larvae of many of the longicorns are formidable wood borers and as such constitute an important force in the cycle of growth and decay in the forest. The larvae have been known to feed in rotten wood for as long as three years before pupating. Upon emerging, the adult switches to flowers and pollen.

CLAWING A BEATER during a hunt in Madhya Pradesh, a tiger wrestles the man to the ground and tears at him with teeth and claws. Tigers can usually be driven by a line of shouting beaters into a position where they can be shot, but sometimes they turn, as this one did. The beater was lucky; he survived—after months in a hospital.

7

Pythons, Rhinos and Others

Almost everybody knows the lively and delightful tales of animals in India which Rudyard Kipling wrote in *The Jungle Book*. It was more than just an accident of colonialism that made this romantic chronicler of Britain's golden age of empire choose India for his locale; the subjects he found there were uniquely suited to his pen. In India, there has developed, through countless generations, a relationship between the wild and the human populations found nowhere else: a blend of mysticism, affection, respect and tolerance, as well as fear, which alone could give rise to such stories as those of Mowgli, the infant boy who was reared by wolves in the midst of jungle life.

And what has become of Mowgli's animal friends in the India of today? Most of them are still there, 60 years after Kipling peopled his pages with them. Akela the wolf, scientifically known as *Canis lupus*, still roams the forests, a somewhat smaller subspecies than his relatives of northern Eurasia and North America. Bagheera, the black panther, is still very much in evidence: this not uncommon mutation of *Panthera pardus* extends from India eastward into Burma and southward into the Malay Peninsula, where, if anything, black panthers are more common than the usual spotted leopard forms. The red dog, or dhole,

A RATTLING PORCUPINE

Although quills are an excellent defense for all porcupines, there is still the chance that an inexperienced predator or other large animal will tangle with one of these prickly animals, and while getting badly stuck itself, will still damage the porcupine by trying to eat it or accidentally treading on it. The next step, therefore, is to advertise that one is prickly and dangerous, and that is what a porcupine of Borneo does. Hystrix crassispinis, shown here, has a cluster of hollow quills with open ends on its tail. When the tail is shaken, they rattle, making a warning noise, and other animals learn to avoid this sound just as they must the warning of an aroused rattlesnake.

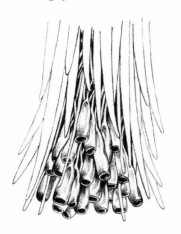

Cuon alpinus, is as fierce and untamable as ever, running in tireless packs that hunt down deer, wild pigs and goats, and even attack bears and tigers, which, if beset by a dhole pack, will surrender their prey as Kipling had them do. Another subspecies, even redder than the Indian form and with a flashing white underside, occurs from Burma to Singapore and on the big islands of Java, Sumatra and Borneo.

And Baloo, the bear who played so avuncular a role in Mowgli's young life? This was in all likelihood a sloth bear, known in India as *bhalu*, though Kipling described his Baloo as brown. Sloth bears have long, straight, black hair and favor rocky places in the jungles throughout India and Ceylon and eastward into Assam. There are also the Asiatic black bears, sometimes known as moon bears, which range from Persia to Assam and northeast through China to Taiwan and Japan, and are distinguished by a broad, white V on their chests. There is the sun bear, black with a strange yellow crescent on its chest and found from Assam to perhaps as far as Szechwan in China, and south through Burma, parts of Indochina and Malaya, and in Sumatra and Borneo.

THESE are all distinctive creatures, stamped somehow with the unmistakable imprint of the Oriental region—but of them all, perhaps the best known is the Indian python, *Python molorus,* the giant snake personified by Kipling as Mowgli's sleepy and affectionate friend Kaa. A close relative of the reticulated python, which has a wider range extending all through Southeast Asia and all of the larger islands as far as the Philippines, this great reptile has stirred men's imaginations since memory began.

The python Kaa ate seldom and slept a great deal, which is just what pythons do. As big as they are—the Indian python reaches 20 feet in length, the reticulated python 33—they can swallow at a single meal many times more than their daily requirement of food, and fasts of as much as a year between meals are not uncommon in captivity. Their prey consists of mammals of suitable size—an 18-foot Indian python was once collected which had the remains of a leopard in its stomach—and birds such as chickens and pheasants. They are singularly unaggressive creatures and make good pets. Along with the far more dangerous cobras, they are the common stock in trade of snake charmers and are often seen in zoos.

As members of the family of Boidae, pythons kill by constriction: having seized their prey in their jaws, they rapidly throw several coils around it and exert enough pressure to prevent chest expansion, thereby causing death from suffocation or heart stoppage. The prey is then simply swallowed in the most convenient manner, a process which may take an hour or more if it is a big animal like a pig or a small deer. Goats may be eaten, horns and all, and even pangolins and porcupines—though the latter on at least one occasion proved fatal to a python, which was found dead with its stomach punctured in many places by the sharp quills. If the prey is a horned animal, the horns are often regurgitated after digestion is accomplished.

Pythons are still common throughout Southeast Asia—the even larger reticulate python of Burma, Indochina and Malaya is occasionally found in cities as well as in the jungle—but another lordly creature has all but vanished today.

In the Gir Forest of the old princely state of Junagadh in western India live the last remnants of India's once-proud race of lions, today among the very rarest of all wild animals in the Oriental region. Lions once ranged over all of northern India except its easternmost extremes and were found as far south as the Nabrada River and the Satpura hills. In the heyday of empire, they were favored game of sportsmen—one hunter killed more than 300 of them, 50 right around Delhi—and by 1884 they were all but exterminated. Today the Gir Forest, a 500-square-mile patch of poor forest and thorn shrub country, is the last refuge for some 250 individuals.

It is a curious fact that relatively little is known even today about the Indian lion, either in a historical or a morphological sense. It is generally believed that this member of the Asiatic race of lions, once widely distributed throughout Asia Minor, Palestine and Arabia as well as India, predates the tiger, which probably entered India from the northeast after the last ice age, but much still remains to be learned of its early distribution. And the simple fact that Indian lions were killed off so fast and in such numbers by big game hunters has precluded any large-scale collection of specimens for morphological studies. As Lee Merriam Talbot puts it in his invaluable book *A Look at Threatened Species:* "A considerable number of specimens must adorn the floors, walls and trunks of present and former officers of the Indian government, Indian royalty and big game hunters. These trophies . . . provide an untapped source of zoological materials." The present population in the Gir Forest is too small and precarious to permit any collecting on an adequate scale. Furthermore, the fact that the lions, running short of their natural prey of antelope, deer and wild pig, have taken to preying on domestic livestock has made them something of a political problem: herdsmen who graze their stock in the forest preserve are resentful of the order forbidding them to take protective measures against the lions.

Lions and tigers are closely related—so much so that in captivity they can sometimes be interbred—but only in Asia do these two big cats live, so to speak, side by side, or at least they did before the lion was hunted nearly to extinction in India. Shere Khan, as Kipling calls the tiger, is still numerous throughout much of the region. There are probably about 4,000 tigers living wild in India, and hunting pressure must still occasionally be brought to bear to keep their numbers down locally. They are also found east to Indochina, in Java, Sumatra and Bali, but not in Ceylon or Borneo. Smaller than the big Siberian or Manchurian tigers, they nonetheless may measure nine feet or more from nose to tip of tail and weigh about 400 pounds.

As dangerous as tigers are in pursuit of their normal prey—antelope, deer, wild pigs, monkeys and, when pressed for food, domestic livestock—they are not by nature man-hunters. The naturalist E. P. Gee in his recent book *The Wild Life of India* described the tiger as "one of the safest and most gentlemanly creatures of the jungle." In support of this he cites a personal experience: "I remember once walking for a mile or more through some tall grass. What was presumably a cow was walking away just in front of me—I could hear it and could see the grass moving as the animal walked ahead. Eventually I came to an open place, and there was the 'cow'—a huge tiger."

Gee's statement is carefully qualified, and with reason: he excepts tigers that are molested by man. Danger immediately arises if a tigress is disturbed with her cubs. And if an old or wounded tiger is no longer able to pursue its normal prey he may turn to eating man.

Since this chapter is concerned with some of the rare and unusual animals with which the Oriental region is stocked like some extraordinary zoo, it seems fitting now to consider the pheasants of Southeast Asia, which include some of the region's most flamboyant birds. Père David, the noted French scientist-priest who recorded so much of the wildlife of China a century ago, mentions finding two of the less common but most beautiful species: the Impeyan pheasant, a shimmering, iridescent, violet-green and gold bird of the hill meadows around 15,000 feet, and the blue-eared pheasant, a species of *Crossoptilon*, which he also found in the mountains of Sikang and Szechwan. They were unusual and valuable finds, for most pheasants occur at lower altitudes and on islands, from Ceylon east to the Greater Sundas, Palawan in the Philippines, Hainan and Taiwan. The Oriental region is their heartland, but they show an ancient tropical link with the isolated evergreen forest of west Africa, a link corroborated by the fact that pheasants occur as Cenozoic fossils in Europe. The two present end habitats were perhaps connected in Miocene times.

My favorite among pheasants is surely the oddest of its kind, *Lophura bulweri*, or Bulwer's pheasant, found in Borneo in lowland jungle. The male's body feathers have iridescent reddish and blue-black reflections and the large tail is pure white and curved into a broad fan shape. The legs are bright red and the eye is ruby red. In display the male's two pairs of three-inch wattles above and below the eye become engorged with blood and turn a flaring cobalt blue completely surrounding the ruby-red eye, which itself becomes brighter, surcharged with blood. The effect is electrifying—a ruby bull's-eye in a cobalt dish.

The puzzle, though, is that despite the gorgeous development of the cock Bulwer's pheasant, presumably to impress the female, this bird has proved to be one of the least successful of its kind in maintaining and expanding its territory in the forest, and is only known from small areas within the island of Borneo. By comparison, the equally elaborate but very different male of the argus pheasant is found not only on the islands but on the continental mainland as well—and is very common over most of its range. So much so that one of the most familiar sounds to the traveler on a river or through the wilderness of the rain forest in these parts is the distinctive, loud, double whistle of this magnificent peacock-sized bird.

The cock argus pheasant goes further still in making itself distinctive, putting on an active dancing display on bare patches of earth in the jungle. The greatest student of pheasants, the late William Beebe, concluded that each ground was occupied by a single male, but the Dayaks of Borneo deny this, saying that several males display competitively in one clearing.

LIKE the pheasants, the monkeys of the Oriental region, too, are part of a chain. The leaf-eating monkeys, the langurs of the Orient and the colobus monkeys, or guerezas, of Africa, belong to a common group found today widely isolated on two continents but linked by Pliocene fossils in Europe. In Africa the colobus monkeys occur in heavy tropical forest or isolated patches of forest. On the other hand, the langurs are found in every sort of habitat from Himalayan snows and the dry, semidesert scrub in western India and northern Ceylon to the cold mountains of China and along the jungle streams of Borneo. Leaf-eating monkeys are noted for their splendid appearance, the common langurs being the typical handsome monkey of India and Ceylon. They are bearded, with fine smooth fur. Their tails are long, longer than the body, and carried gracefully arched and curled high as they run across the ground or leap, sometimes 25 feet out and as much as 40 feet down, through the trees. They are great talkers, the langurs, and often warn the hunter of the presence of tiger or leopard by guttural shouts and cries. Their one implacable enemy is the leopard—but leopards do not go hungry in Indian forests. As the bear Baloo told Mowgli, the "Bandar-log," or Monkey-People, can never remember anything for long—and sooner or later a langur will forget or make a mistake and the leopard will have another meal.

Another most unusual animal, the dugong, is found in the warm seas of the Oriental region as well as along the east coast of Africa and the northern shores of Australia. My first introduction to it was in the museum at Aden at the foot of the Red Sea, where I spent sixpence to see the "mermaids." Sure enough, ensconced in three enormous boxes like coffins lay the bodies of three stuffed dugongs, or sea cows. The stuffing had made them even more grotesque than they are in life and the taxidermist had been at pains to increase their resemblance to mermaids or mermen by emphasizing the generative organ of the male and the breasts of the females. It is said that the mother dugong clasps her baby to her breast with her "arms," or front flippers, but this seems implausible. Anyone who has ever seen a live dugong mother with a baby has noted that the baby clings to the mother's back as she browses through the shoals of sea grass and other marine plants on which the creatures feed, and furthermore the breast is directly under the flipper, as if in the armpit, and the young probably reach round and suckle from the back.

Poor dugongs. Modified over eons of time for a harmless grazing life in shallow, warm seas, equipped with tails but no hind limbs, heavy and cumbersome and full of blubbery fat, useful to the local human inhabitants wherever they live, the species seems doomed to certain extinction. The inoffensive creatures have been speared or caught in nets, cut up, and the meat and hide sold and the blubber boiled down for oil. A 600-pound dugong will yield from six to 14 gallons of oil. The range of ailments treated with dugong oil is startling: it is said to be efficacious for dysentery as well as constipation, good for head- or earaches and useful in treating all manner of skin diseases. No wonder that dugongs are hunted. Even the tears of the dugong, which it sheds copiously when it is brought out of the salt water, have a commercial value. Although they are nothing but a mucous secretion which probably helps to protect the eyes by converting the excess salt sea water into wastes, as it is in seabirds, they are considered potent as a love charm by Malayan fishermen, another inducement to capture the animals. One can only hope that protection will soon be afforded these clumsy, harmless distant relatives of elephants and hyraxes before they vanish from the scene.

The armored pangolin belongs to a special family, found in the Oriental region and in tropical Africa, with Pleistocene fossil relatives in southern India, and a giant species in Java and Borneo, which, on the latter island, existed until a mere 50,000 years ago. A typical Asiatic pangolin is a humped-looking creature from two to three and a half feet long, weighing up to 17 pounds, with a small, narrow, pointed head ending in almost immovable jaws, and a tiny mouth from which a sticky 10-inch tongue may protrude if there are any ants or termites about. The beast is completely covered above with large horny scales but nearly naked below, the skin covered with scanty hair. The scale-covered tail is nearly half as long as the body and head and slightly prehensile. In the female the tail forms an efficient seat on which one or two babies can ride. Pangolins walk on their front knuckles, the powerful claws turned inward. With these claws they can burrow into the hardest of termite nests or excavate their own dens in which parents and young live as much as 12 feet below ground, often between large boulders to discourage interference by human or other

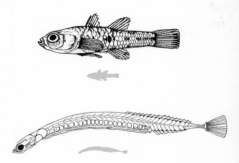

THE WORLD'S SMALLEST

No matter whether they are measured by size or weight, the smallest fishes in the world live in tropical Asian waters. The shortest fish, and in fact the shortest known vertebrate, is Pandaka pygmaea (above), a one-third-inch bantam from the Philippines. Somewhat longer but even lighter is Schindleria praematurus. A thousand of these midgets weigh less than a dime. They are completely transparent except for the black pigment of their eyes and their swim bladders, and are extremely difficult to see, although they sometimes swarm in shallow New Guinea waters in countless numbers. Actual sizes of these fishes are indicated by the small silhouettes shown in color.

predators. For of course the horny scales, like other horny constructions, are considered to have a medicinal value among some peoples in the Orient, particularly the Chinese, and pangolins have been much preyed on by humans. Pangolins feed on termites and ants especially. They are fond of almost any species; if a pangolin is at work in a nest of the biting red ant, sometimes well up in a tree, it will pause every so often to remove them from its face or abdomen by scratching vigorously. The pangolin has a throat gland, the use of which may be connected with the powerful salivary glands, which keep the tongue mucous and sticky. Pangolins kept in captivity drink water and milk, using the long tongue dexterously for lapping up the liquid and often darting it in and out so rapidly as to beat up a froth.

The naturalist W.W.A. Phillips tells a story of the immense strength of a pangolin in Ceylon. The creatures roll themselves into a very effective horny ball when frightened or anxious to protect themselves. Not realizing this, a villager clubbed a pangolin one day in the jungle and started back for his home, the animal slung over his neck, the tail hanging down on one side, the head on the other. But the beast was merely stunned. When found later, the man was dead on the trail, strangled. The pangolin had apparently suddenly come to life and had automatically coiled itself round his neck in its defensive posture. The creature was still curled tightly round the villager's neck, proving that he was the victim of a scaly mugging.

M Y own favorites among the rare animals of the Orient are the three species of rhinoceros. The family to which they belong is old as large mammals go and probably arose in Eurasia about 52 million years ago, from whence it spread to North America and Africa. The smallest living Asiatic species is the Sumatran, perhaps four and a half feet high at the shoulder, eight to nine feet long, weighing up to 2,000 pounds and distinguished by a rather hairy coat. The two other Asian rhinos are both much larger and more like each other in appearance. There is the great Indian rhinoceros, a huge armored beast, more than six feet at the shoulder, 14 feet long and probably weighing as much as two tons. The second, slightly smaller animal is the Javan rhinoceros, six inches or so lower at the shoulder and much lighter in weight, probably just over one ton. All three rhinoceroses are now very limited in range. Formerly found from Bengal east through Burma to Vietnam and south into Sumatra and Java, the Javan rhinoceros is found today only in the Udjung Kulon Reserve on an uninhabited peninsula on the western tip of Java. According to the latest information available, there now may be only about 25 individuals left in this area, which would mean this once abundant animal is in imminent peril of extinction.

The essential rhino problem is that the horn and other parts of the body are highly touted and valued in Oriental medicine. Powdered rhinoceros horn is a specific in the Asian medical lore for everything from impotence to removing thorns, easing labor pains, shrinking lumps, as an antiseptic, for closing cuts or even for mending broken bones. Every part of the rhino has its price—horns are worth up to $200 or more per ounce—and there is even said to be an obscure Indian religious rite, a sort of purge, performed by squatting inside the body cavity of a freshly killed rhino after it has been eviscerated. Certain prayers are recited and the severed rhino horn is used as a cup to hold the rhino blood offered to the gods. Even rhino urine is valuable. As recently as the 1950s a zoo in Asia made a welcome income of over $2,000 a year selling rhino urine from its captive pair of great Indians.

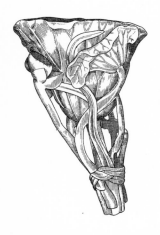

LEGENDARY CUPS OF HORN

Rhinoceros horn cups, delicately hand-carved as shown here, are the source of many romantic Oriental legends. One is that they would shatter if they contained poison. Because rhinoceros horn, unlike that of most other mammals, is actually made of compacted hair, the cup may have warned, but in a way less dramatic than the legend. Since many ancient poisons were strong alkaloids, they no doubt separated the hair strands of the horn, causing noticeable disintegration inside of the cup and thus alerting the owner.

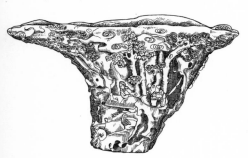

The Indian rhino now lives only in one area of Nepal, along the foothills of the Himalayas in forest and grassland near rivers, and in eastern India in Bengal and Assam, mostly in open, swampy reserves or sanctuaries. There are perhaps 600 left, as well as 30 in zoos, including a few pairs that have successfully produced offspring.

The small Sumatran rhino occurs from the lowlands to over 6,000 feet, in dense jungle in a thin, attenuated range that may harbor perhaps 170 individuals. Some are scattered in mountainous parts of Burma, a very few in Malaya, probably none in Thailand or Vietnam, possibly 20 in Sumatra and an equal number in the mountainous areas of Borneo between the Indonesian territory and the Sarawak-North Borneo side. They are virtually never seen, certainly not by any outsider. One of the Americans who has been attempting to survey Malaya and Sumatra for the remaining Sumatran rhinos caught two glimpses of two individual Sumatran rhinoceroses in five months work in 1961. Both sightings were in dense jungle, one for a few seconds, one for several minutes as the sound of a stream drowned out the noise he made walking up to the animal. Blessed with keen hearing and sense of smell, the rhinoceros in the jungle is very wary. One of its few giveaways is the presence of wallows. All three Asian species like to wallow at least once a day in a muddy hole, sometimes on the side of a steep hill, perhaps where a tree has been uprooted. The muddy liquid must be soothing and perhaps helps get rid of parasites such as leeches and unwelcome insects. But wallows are an indication of the presence of the animals and so a danger for them.

My study of these creatures has centered around the Indian rhinoceros in Assam. At the request of the Assam state forestry officials, an Indian colleague, Dr. Sálim Ali, and I spent many fascinating days in 1949 plodding about the swamps along the Brahmaputra River, looking for rhinos. As a result some estimate of the numbers of the species could be made and some observations on their habits as well. The Indian Government authorities are anxious to make the 166-square-mile Kaziranga Sanctuary, where nearly 300 rhinoceroses are thought to live, into a tourist attraction. Eventually it is hoped visitors from all over India, as well as foreigners, will be able to catch a glimpse of a wild rhinoceros, one of the last great archaic-looking species of mammal, a link with vanished epochs and vanished faunas.

ONE of the results of our observations pointed toward a difficulty in all this. A rhinoceros lives to be about 50 years old. It is presumed adult at 12 to 15 years, and the gestation period in the female is approximately 19 months. Thus a female of adult age can breed, assuming she feeds her calf for at least six to 10 months, only every three years or so. Rhinos in captivity have proved very difficult to breed, as both male and female appear to come into breeding condition separately at varying seasons and their seasons do not necessarily coincide. In addition, the great Indian rhinoceros is normally very unsociable. Individuals, males or females, at Kaziranga choose out a particular territory. One animal will occupy perhaps 20 to 50 acres, marked by one or more wallows and irregular trails extending to a water hole or some open grazing land. More important, the territory appears to be marked out by heaps of dung, one near the center of the territory, others along the trails and near the wallows. These heaps are often three feet high and several feet across and are maintained by the animal backing up to the pile so as not to tread it down.

But the rhinoceros does not always stay on its territory. In March, one of the several times that we were in Kaziranga, there were notably few rhinos to be found. As near as I can conclude, March is a likely time of year for breeding activity of this seasonally variable animal. The absence of several individuals and the coincident report of wandering, sometimes several hundred miles away, even of individuals swimming across the Brahmaputra, inclines me to the supposition that the rhinoceros, territorial most of the year, has a wandering period during the time of sexual activity when it seeks out a mate. We noticed that the rhino appears to have a different call associated with mating, a high penetrating whistle. All of this may explain the occasional appearance of rhinos far away from their known haunts. It may also explain how the small Sumatran rhino manages to persist. This is also an unsociable species and would appear to be a tremendous wanderer. Even if there are only a dozen Sumatran rhinoceroses in a thousand miles of tumbled hills and ridges of northern Burma, it may be possible for these creatures to work north and south along their game trails and occasionally encounter each other. This may account for the known disappearance and reappearance of these incredibly rugged will-o'-the-wisp creatures from thousands of square miles of forest land over a period of years. If this wandering is a necessary component of the survival of the species, it makes the whole problem of protection vastly more complicated, even though it also makes poaching difficult.

TWO WAYS TO HIDE

A Malayan tapir at different stages in its life has two distinct types of protective coloration. The baby is dark brown with tawny spots and streaks, and blends into the sun- or moon-dappled forest floor. The adult animal has a coat of contrasting areas of black and white. In the jungle night the white midsection of the nocturnal tapir does not suggest the form of an entire animal, since the black of the head, shoulders and legs remains obscure. With the lines of the tapir disrupted, night-prowling tigers and other predators often fail to recognize it as prey.

PERHAPS even more of a mystery than the rhino is the Malayan tapir, the rhino's cousin. Now found as a single species in southern Burma, Thailand, Malaya and Sumatra, it has been extinct in Borneo since historic times. The tapir of Asia is a lumbering black and white creature which has been around since the Cenozoic but has relatives today only in Central and South America. Harmless, incredibly keen of sight, smell and hearing, the tapir persists in dense evergreen jungle by its senses alone. It is easily killed by leopards, tigers or wild dogs, but its natural enemies fortunately do not include man. For some reason the tapir is largely taboo. In southern Burma it is not hunted because it is thought by some to have a semireligious mystical quality. In Malaya some people feel that to eat the flesh brings on leprosy. Fortunately sportsmen do not shoot it because it makes a poor trophy: with no tusks or other prominent appendages, a mounted head merely looks silly. As someone once said in the Rangoon *Gazette:* "It [the tapir] is a perpetual refutation of the general application of theories on the struggle for existence. It is a shy and mild and gentle creature. It is easily tamed in captivity. It is nothing much to look at and its white overcoat is an amusing vagary of jungle fashion. The female is bigger than the male. A small shrill squeal is the only sound recorded in connection with the animal. . . . It is not poached, the jungle people regarding it as is the fate of many philosophers living out of their time with 'almost amused contempt.' . . . The tapir is in fact an enigma. It may be a survivor of some more gentle and legendary time, or it may be wandering in unique isolation in a world not yet mature enough for its wisdom."

An interesting group of animals in the Oriental region is that of the pigs. The wild boar of Europe, *Sus scrofa,* ancestor of domestic hogs, has its relatives right through southern Asia in the wild pigs of China and Japan south to Formosa. *Sus scrofa cristatus,* the powerful crested pig of India and Southeast Asia, is closely related to the wild boar but has a more prominent mane, while the whitish streak on the cheek is less pronounced. In ancient times these pigs were evidently domesticated and it was probably some form of the wild boar and/or crested pig which was brought by early man into the islands east of Java and Borneo. A number of subspecies of wild pig have been described from Celebes and the Lesser Sunda Islands east to Timor, the Moluccas and New Guinea, but present-day authorities believe that some are feral relics of man's importations. Not so the bearded pig, a huge creature found in Borneo and Malaya and little known even today. The bearded pig has whitish, curly whiskers and a huge, wartlike, bristle-covered growth on the snout. The oddest member of the pig family is of course the babirussa, mentioned in an earlier chapter, from Celebes and the islands to the east.

Smallest of all the pigs is the pygmy hog, *Sus salvanius*, described by the pioneer naturalist Bryan Hodgson in 1847. This little pig may or may not be extinct. There is no reliable record of anyone seeing it in recent years, but it is quite possible that the pygmy hog hangs on in small numbers in the Terai district of Nepal and perhaps farther to the northwest.

Cattle and sheep are primarily Old World, and large cattle are an important component of the Oriental region. The water buffalo was probably first domesticated about 5,000 years ago in India, from where it spread to Iran and then to the Balkan Peninsula, Italy and the southern shores of the Mediterranean in the Middle Ages. Today these huge and useful animals occur from eastern Europe and Egypt to China and south into the Sunda Islands as far south and east as northern Australia, where feral animals, descendants of domestic stock, occur. Wild water buffalo still occur in India and Ceylon, but are probably extinct in most of their former eastern range or exist only as feral remnant herds. In either case, they are not nearly as savage as the African species, to which they are closely related.

The gaur, called seladang in Malaya, is a superb species of wild ox still found in south India, Nepal, Assam, Burma, Malaya and parts of Vietnam. A herd of gaur is one of the sights of south India. This tremendous animal may stand more than six feet at the shoulder and may weigh over 2,000 pounds. A close relative is the smaller banteng of Burma, Malaya and the Greater Sunda Islands. These two wild oxen are unique in the Oriental region, with no really close relatives elsewhere in the world. Perhaps the only relative anywhere is the other wild ox of Southeast Asia, the kouprey, or forest ox, of Cambodia. Known only from small scattered herds totaling perhaps 1,000 altogether, this big gray ox, with curiously frayed horns and a prominent dewlap hanging below the neck like domestic Brahma or Zebu cattle, may be an ancestor of the domesticated breeds of India or it may be an isolated feral relict of the vanished Khmer civilization of Angkor.

THE kouprey is now confined to the forest glades of Cambodia in two separate regions, some 150 miles apart, on opposite sides of the Mekong River. Perhaps the most remarkable thing about this animal is that it only became known to the outside world in 1937, when it was first discovered for science. This illustrates how much may remain to be discovered, even in the comparatively open and easy country in that part of Indochina.

Cattle do strange and provocative things genetically. The gayal, a small version of the gaur, appears to be purely a domesticated form of that huge wild ox, with shorter, straighter horns. Chin tribesmen of the Burma-East Pakistan border hills claim that gayals are the result of inbreeding of an original cross between a wild gaur and a domestic cow, and that after the fourth generation they breed true. The Mishmi, Dafhla and Naga hill tribes in the Tirap frontier areas where I have traveled keep gayals as a half-savage, half-domesticated species. The *mithan*, as the animals are called there, are used as symbols of family prestige and sacrificed at special family or clan feasts by wealthy tribesmen as part of the ascent of the prestige or social ladder. Do they—or did they ever—interbreed with gaurs? Even professional mammalogists are not sure—much research remains to be undertaken by future generations of geneticists before we can be sure of the relationships and historical evolution of the wild cattle and their relatives.

The goat antelopes are a group closely allied to cattle. One species, the serow, which looks rather like a small, blackish Rocky Mountain goat, is found in the Himalayas and thence east to Malaya, southwest China and Sumatra. These goat antelopes are found on wooded cliff faces in the roughest, steepest country and stand about three feet at the shoulder with a prominent mane. They may weigh nearly 200 pounds. One of the few serows I ever saw was in the high plateau area of Mount Loser in north Sumatra. One of our Dayak assistants and I had a glimpse of a serow around a boulder on the south cliff face at about 9,000 feet above sea level. We were standing quite still looking out over the jungle below when a serow started coming round the boulder to our right. It made merely the slightest scratching noise on the rock ledge and dislodged a pebble or two. The creature stopped, gave us a long look with its intelligent liquid eyes and then backed away round the boulder again, the only sensible thing it could do at the time.

THERE are two smaller relatives of the serow, one from Japan and Formosa not much more than half the size of the Sumatran species, and the equally small goral, a goat antelope of the Himalayas. The oddest of the serow's relatives is much larger. This is the takin, a rather oxlike creature found in the Mishmi Hills of northeast Assam, far northern Burma and up into west China in Sikang, Szechwan and Shensi. Its heavy, shaggy fur gives the takin the look of a small cow or yak. The horns measure up to 24 inches in length and are almost lyre-shaped, rising up, then sweeping outward and back and up again. Takin live in heavy forest on the steepest hillsides and scrabble about on tiny splayed hoofs almost as efficiently as their serow cousins, in spite of their far heavier fur and clumsy appearance. I never managed to see one in the Mishmi Hills although several times we saw trails and spoor and were close enough behind to smell the beast's characteristic, very strong, musky odor.

The takin lives in those wonderful clean hills high up, in a world of rhododendron, magnolia and bamboo, where gentians, lilies and blue or yellow poppies star the exposed grassy meadows. Blood pheasants, green and red, or tragopans, gray, spotted-crimson and blue, take wing in front of you, the sun striking sparks from their brilliant raiment. All round above the cliffs, dotted with clumps of larch, sometimes of dwarf maples, dwarf rhododendrons, yew and tiny, twisted oaks, rise higher hills and yet higher, patched with dazzling fields of snow merging into towering castles of cloud. Far below, in the steep valleys, lie solid banks of deodar, cedar and pine, below them the varied tones of the heavier jungle and below that again a glimpse of the serpentine sheen of a river, patches of cultivation, a scarred slope of old slash-and-burn, and here and there the smoke of a tribal fire. This is the most romantic country in the world for a naturalist, the mountainous, ribbed heartland of southern Asia where the variety of animals ranging from valley to ridge to valley challenges the imagination. Here evolution seems to be at work before one's eyes.

COOLING OFF ON A HOT DAY, AN INDIAN TIGER SWIMS IN A BANGALORE STREAM. UNLIKE MOST CATS, IT HAS NO FEAR OF THE WATER

Beasts of Royalty

Closely associated with people for many centuries before civilization spread westward, Asian elephants and rhinos are more tractable than those in Africa. Both have been the favorites of Indian kings, the tuskers as steeds and servants, and the one-horned behemoths as "tanks" in battle or as royal game. But the secluded tiger—also prized quarry—remains as wild as its jungle sanctuary.

TRAILING A MAN-EATER, 500 beaters set out with spears from a village in Assam. Wounded by a hunter eight months earlier and unable to pursue its natural prey, the tiger had killed 35 people.

The Death of a Red "Goddess"

Its growl the fury of the goddess Devi, its coat the color of flame in the tall grass, the tiger is both feared and revered in India. Due to the scarcity of wild game, many individuals have become cattle killers, and perhaps three or four in a thousand are man-eaters. Exterminating one of these is usually a job for a professional hunter, who may spend several weeks finding its trail, setting out live bait under a machan, or tree platform, and waiting for the trespasser to come within range of his gun. Less commonly, a big tiger shoot is organized under the aegis of a prince, and the quarry is surrounded by trained elephants or driven by beaters toward the hunter. In modern India, a license is required to shoot a tiger, and the price of the hunt is high—from $2,000 to $2,500.

AT THE CLIMAX OF THE HUNT, the tiger is chased into a V-shaped net which is closed by the beaters and drawn tighter *(left)* until the desperate animal charges and dies at spear point *(above)*.

155

Rescuing the Rhino

Somewhat less obstreperous than its African relatives, the great Indian rhinoceros may learn to tolerate people in the wild and even becomes docile in captivity. Some of the ancient kings trained rhinos for warfare, placing them in the front lines, with iron tridents on their horns. The horn is apparently not used as a weapon; when a rhino charges, it tries to gash an opponent with its tushes—long lower incisors. The decline of this once numerous species began about 350 years ago during the Mogul dynasty, due to cultivation of the lowlands and the rising human population. At the turn of the 20th Century the survivors, in the northeastern hill country, were hard pressed by hunting for sport and for profit. Now protected in eight sanctuaries in Bengal, Assam and Nepal, the rhinos number about 600. Some 16 individuals have been trapped and shipped to zoos during the past decade, and more may soon be transferred to a new preserve in Nepal.

WALLOWING in a swampy pond, a great Indian rhino is observed from elephant-back in Kaziranga Sanctuary, Assam. From a dozen, in 1908, the number has grown to nearly 300.

A RHINO IS TRAPPED in a pit dug along one of its accustomed paths and camouflaged. As shown above, it must be subdued with lassoes, which then guide the animal as it climbs out.

ALMOST CAGED, the exhausted rhino collapses on the ramp and is cooled with a can of water. An elephant will haul the cage and its occupant, weighing about two tons, to a stockade.

A JAVAN RHINO, one of the rarest sights in the world, dines on twigs and leaves of saplings which it has pushed down in the tropical forest. The female's horn, as shown here, is vestigial, but the male's averages 10 inches. This rhino is the scarcest of the three Asian species, its total population now reduced to about 25 individuals in the Udjung Julon Reserve. Since very few calves have been seen in recent years, naturalists fear the adults are too few and scattered for successful breeding.

COMMEMORATING DASARA, a fall festival of the triumph of good over evil, artists decorate an elephant in Mysore. It is freshly painted each day.

Once upon an Elephant

Domesticated as early as the cow, the Indian elephant was probably a riding animal by 2500 B.C., and in Medieval times carried Oriental potentates on its magnificently caparisoned back in state ceremonies. The elephants most in demand for the great processions, which still mark some holidays, belonged to a large and powerful breed, the Koomeriah. Rare albinos, prized above all, were held sacred by Buddhists and Hindus; the king himself could not ride a "white elephant."

The war elephant originated in Asia, where a ruler's power was reckoned by the number he put into the field. Elephants bore the crossbowmen of Kublai Khan and the archers and musketeers of Akbar, greatest of Mogul emperors, to victory against Hindu princes. But gunpowder frightened the animals, causing them to break and scatter their ranks; by 1700, elephant divisions were becoming outmoded. The last one was demobilized in the Kingdom of Annam in 1882.

WITH SILVER ANKLETS fastened as a final decoration, the Maharaja of Mysore's elephant is readied to receive royal homage, or "puja," on the ninth day of Dasara, when Hindus honor all the animals that serve them.

THE MOGUL AKBAR, A GREAT TAMER OF WILD ELEPHANTS, RACES ACROSS THE JHELUM RIVER, SCATTERING SUBJECTS IN HIS WAKE

DIRECTED BY A MAHOUT, A BIG TUSKER HANDLES A TEAK LOG ALMOST AS EFFORTLESSLY AS A BRANCH. IT FELLS TREES AND LIFTS LOGS WEIGHIN

The Life of a Worker

Even today, as jets fly overhead and automobiles ply the roads, there are about 3,000 working elephants in India and nearby countries. Compared with machines, elephants seem inefficient; they require extensive training, have limited endurance and consume mountains of rice. But they can do some jobs better. Apart from hauling timber and carrying merchandise from one market center to another, elephants are now used to plow farmlands, at half the cost of operating tractors. In a few months, a mahout, assisted by tame elephants, teaches a new recruit some 30 commands which it never forgets. In return, the animal is required to labor only four hours a day and grazes free three months of the year.

A TON, AND DRAGS LOADS UP TO TWO TONS

SHARING A TRUNKFUL of water with his elephant, a mahout refreshes himself during a working day in Nepal. The relationship between an elephant and its trainer is close and may last the animal's lifetime.

8

The Human Invasion

MAN as a component creature of the Oriental region deserves a place in any discussion of the flora and fauna there for two important reasons. The first is concerned with his origins. Nobody knows as yet where and in what manner the gap was bridged which separates man from the primates, but we do know that very important developments in that phase of our evolution took place in tropical Asia. At the end of the 19th Century, when men of learning everywhere were still arguing hotly about Darwin's theory of evolution, a fossil find of the utmost importance was made in Java—the skull and thighbone of a creature which stood apparently midway between ape and man and which lent incontrovertible support to Darwin's proposition that man, like all other living things, had evolved through natural selection from lower species. This was *Pithecanthropus erectus*, so named by its finder, Eugene Dubois, from the Greek words for "erect ape-man." For a good many years after that, until even more ancient finds were made in Africa, it was the oldest of man's ancestors found anywhere.

The second important reason for studying man in tropical Asia is that he exists there today in a diversity of races unmatched anywhere else on earth.

Malays and Mongoloids, Negritos and Australoids and Caucasoids in all their many mixtures have given the local populations an aspect as bewildering to the visitor as it is fascinating to the anthropologist. This is a place where multiple invasions taking place over thousands of years have changed man, his culture and his environment time and time again, so that tracing his history there results in a complicated story, a story which repeatedly draws the student off on tantalizing tangents and flashbacks like a historical novel told on a gigantic scale.

Perhaps, too, there is a third reason which cannot as yet be documented at all. There is a very dim period in the history of man, beginning sometime after the early hominids evolved, of which we know almost nothing—a time when these creatures were first applying and developing the freedom found when they learned to walk erect, used their hands and brains to shape tools, and began to consider the world around them. In this period some of the groups of hominids died out, while others survived, spread out and slowly began to dominate the world. One such race gave rise to the Neanderthals, which were pre-eminent in Eurasia 75,000 to 50,000 years ago, only to disappear suddenly for unknown reasons. So far, no comparable hominid development has been discovered in Southeast Asia—but this does not mean that there never was one. So the study of man there is always open to the fascinating possibility that someday some new find will shed light on this time of darkness.

Meanwhile, some very important conclusions can be drawn from the existence of *Pithecanthropus erectus* and more recent discoveries of other human types made in the Southeast Asian region.

J AVA man, as *Pithecanthropus erectus* is more commonly known, probably lived some 400,000 or 500,000 years ago. Several million years earlier, in the Pliocene epoch, there were advanced primates, perhaps related to the human stemline in the transition from ape to man, in eastern Africa and Europe, in northern India and in southwestern China. We know this from fossil finds made in these areas. What is particularly intriguing is the similarity of these widely separated forms. Though they are still more ape than man, they resemble each other in various ways so that one can only conclude that they were commonly interconnected or distributed. In other words, there must have been a faunal interchange between these antecedent species from the waist of Africa and Egypt across Europe, and presumably across Southwest Asia to India and China as well.

The earliest manlike creatures found in tropical Asia came to light sometime after the discovery of Java man in a collection of skulls and other bones found in eastern Java and dating back more than 600,000 years ago. These fossils of species thought to have come from tropical south China were both older and more primitive than those of Java man. They were found in what is known locally as the Djetis zone of animal remains in Java. The recent studies of the German paleontologist G.H.R. von Koenigswald on these fragments, especially the teeth, incline him to the belief that these were early *Pithecanthropus* types. The fossils of Java man, also probably from south China, were found in the so-called Trinil zone of central Java, dating back some 500,000 years. Stone flake tools found in this general area indicate that these early men had been toolmakers for some time. They had roughly contemporary relatives living in China. The Chinese cousin was Peking man, whose remains have been found in caves associated with fire and with crude stone tools—chopping tools that were made from large individual quartz or quartzite pebbles, also small stones roughly flaked to a cutting edge.

It is surprising how much of the look of this man can be put together from the bony remains. Java man was about five feet six inches tall; Peking man, slightly smaller, stood five feet one and a half inches or so. The head was well forward but still carried erect on massive neck muscles, and the skull was tremendously thick and heavy, the brain capacity of Peking man being almost as great as the human minimum today. Most anthropologists feel that tools imply some form of communication, and with it memory and the awakening of tradition. Certainly the skull capacities of both Java man and Peking man could allow for this. The conclusion that may perhaps be drawn from comparison with the remains in the Chinese caves was that, having already developed the use of tools, Java man was using them for hunting. Thus he was intimately associated with the animals around him, depending on them for sustenance, consciously and with a growing cleverness pursuing them, pitting his awakening wits against their superior strength and agility.

From the zoogeographic point of view it is important to note that similar jaw or skull fragments of men who lived about that same time have been found in Germany near Heidelberg and in East and North Africa. Clearly, Java man was not alone upon this earth in Southeast Asia.

Today we can put together a little bit about the world these early men lived in, from before 600,000 to perhaps some 500,000 or 400,000 years ago, and how they may have subsisted in it. It was a world rich in animal types, many now extinct on Java although perhaps still found on other islands nearby. One such was the orangutan, which occurred on Java down to this period and then became extinct there, as it did at the same time on the mainland in southern China. Orangutan teeth, especially of young animals, are so common in the Chinese caves and in other caves of later epochs in Borneo that the only valid conclusion seems to be that man was fond of eating these mammals. Java and Peking man also ate monkeys, wild pigs, bamboo rats, tapirs and the present wild ox, the banteng. Peking man was apparently capable of killing deer, sheep, buffalo and bison; remains also indicate that he hunted rhinoceros and elephant, as well as the giant panda. He also, apparently, was not above practicing cannibalism. The condition of the human leg bones and skulls, broken open with crushing tools to get at the marrow or brains, shows this quite clearly.

By the Upper Pleistocene, several hundred thousand years later, we come to another man in Java, related to *Pithecanthropus*, called Solo man after the river near which his fossil bones were found. They are dated 75,000 to 35,000 years ago. Associated with him are remains of two types of elephants, a modern elephant like those still found on the mainland but extirpated from Java 50,000 years ago, and *Stegodon*, a more ancient mastodonlike species. On an island of relatively limited extent, like Java, it appears more than likely that these elephants were hastened to their doom by these early men. Similarly, the miniature elephants of Celebes and the Philippines can be presumed to have become extinct from hunting pressure. What pleasure has been lost to us! What fun it would have been to have been able to look at a full-grown elephant which stood only four feet high at the shoulder!

From about 50,000 years ago onward we are in the Upper Paleolithic, which corresponds to the closing phase of the last Pleistocene glaciation. This stage lasted until what we now call the Recent epoch, beginning some 12,000 to 14,000 years ago. The impression of southern Asia during this time is of a serene and relatively undisturbed climate. This is startling to students of Paleolithic conditions in Europe, northern Africa and North America, who sense in their historical research major climatic changes due to the advance of the glaciers and the polar icecap. In the tropics of Asia, however, the impression derived from the faunal remains is one of equatorial stability affected only by rises and falls in the surrounding seas. The life of Upper to Late Paleolithic was close to what it is today.

Much has been learned of these times within the last decade through the systematic exploration of some of the extensive limestone cave systems found in the islands of tropical Asia, particularly on Borneo. Caves form an ideal repository for early remains: to animals and humans alike they offered shelter, and later, when human populations took to building their own houses and settling elsewhere, the caves were often still used as burial places for their dead. Thus, over thousands of years, evidence of past cultures and creatures was built up in successive layers of debris on the cave floors in these high, dry places. As in the seven cities of Troy, scientists are able to dig down, layer by layer, progressing ever further back through time to reconstruct a picture of the life that existed in the area.

ONE such extensive cave system is near Niah, in Sarawak, in western Borneo. High in the hills rising from the coastal plain, the caves, opening on sheer cliff walls overlooking a swampy valley, are protected from river floods during the monsoon season and from the eroding effects of wind and water. In the dry, cool mouths of the caves, bones have not fossilized but have lain undisturbed with artifacts and other materials, while the slowly accumulating dust of the millennia has covered them.

Caves were more than just a natural refuge for early man. The labyrinth in the Niah limestone massif not only gave man protection from rain and wild beasts but also offered him a source of food in the numerous cave snakes, bats, birds and monitor lizards. Thus the Niah caves were a logical place to look for evidence of man's evolution. And indeed, scientists from the Sarawak Museum have in recent years found here increasing evidence of early civilizations—enough to begin to reconstruct a more complete picture of man in this area than was previously possible. Perhaps it may eventually be possible to find evidence of a civilization comparable to that of Neanderthal man. At least, there are those who hope so.

The first breakthrough in this new direction came in 1958 with the discovery by Tom Harrisson of a skull deep down in the excavation in the 27-acre floor of the Great Cave at Niah. This skull, when its details were published by Donald R. Brothwell of the British Museum, proved beyond doubt to be that of a *Homo sapiens* type—and carbon dating established its age as something between 35,000 and 40,000 years. It was a sensational find, since it tended to pull the supports out from under some previous beliefs about the origin of *Homo sapiens* elsewhere. The prevailing idea was that he had got his start at about that time either in Africa or Eurasia and then spread very slowly. But for him to show up suddenly in Borneo, clearly his origins would have to be pushed back or his rate of dispersal speeded up. The latter idea—that there were a good many more specimens of *Homo sapiens* around than anyone had previously suspected—received apparent confirmation from further cave exploration.

This time the work was on the Philippine island of Palawan, and it brought to light a *sapiens* skull that is probably 20,000 years old.

Looking at man, his history and his works in the light of these finds, an entirely new school of thought must be taken into account—one which embraces the concept that contemporary man existed here in a fairly advanced state of development long before the invasion of outside influences from the west and from the north. Looked at in this way, the astonishing diversity of Southeast Asian peoples makes better sense than it previously did. Instead of looking only for the histories of invading populations, we can seek clues in a human past intimately related to the region itself—and it is here that the story unfolding in the Niah caves attains perhaps its greatest significance. For what is coming to light is a history of multiple impacts of migrations upon *existing* populations over tens of thousands of years, and thereby some of the real riddles of man's past in tropical Asia may slowly be explained.

The potentialities of the Niah caves as a documentary of man's past have been known for some time. According to local legend, they were discovered by a native around 1830. Some 25 years later, Alfred Russel Wallace heard of them during his stay in Sarawak and focused attention on them as a possible site in the search for a Borneo "missing link." But a systematic exploration was not undertaken until 1954, when the museum archeologists dug their first trial trench in the west mouth of the Great Cave. This entrance to the magnificent cathedral-like cavern was chosen because it offered no inducement for man to have disturbed it in modern times—it is too light to provide a haven for edible bats or the little swiftlets that build edible birds' nests. True, natives regularly have gathered the guano and nests from the more than two million bats and birds living in the darker recesses of the cave, but the entrance has not been affected by this activity. And the precipitous approach to the mouth some 150 feet up the cliff from below has prevented wild animals like deer and pigs from wandering in to disrupt the floor. Yet its great size—the mouth here is about 800 feet wide and over 200 feet high—indicated that in the remote past it might have been a major human habitation. And so indeed it proved to be: under a top surface that indicated nothing at all, the very first trial trench brought to light a rich deposit of human materials.

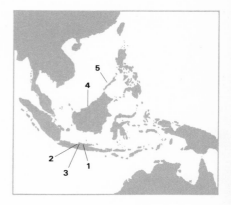

EARLY TRACES OF MAN

Tropical Asia is one of the richest grounds for the fossils and artifacts of man's earliest ancestors. The skullcap of a baby, one of the oldest human fossils ever discovered, was found in the Djetis beds of Java (1). The tiny human was alive more than 600,000 years ago. The first fossil of Pithecanthropus erectus, or Java man, was unearthed in Trinil, Java (2), where it may have rested for 400,000 or 500,000 years. Another Java fossil, Solo man (3), dates back as far as 75,000 years. In the Great Cave in Borneo were found some of the earliest known remnants of modern man, Homo sapiens (4), going back about 40,000 years. Early Homo sapiens remains recently excavated in the Philippines (5) date back about 20,000 years.

THIS is the most startling fact about the west mouth of the Great Cave: what appears at first to be earth, producing a wide, pleasant floor, is really almost solid human deposit reaching back at least into Middle Paleolithic times. The outer part of the mouth was used only sporadically in the Neolithic, mainly for funeral ceremonies and burials—by that time people were already making permanent dwellings out in the rain forest—but in the earlier phases of the Stone Age, in Paleolithic-Mesolithic times, this area was used for regular habitation, evidences of which are piled layer upon layer even at the quite considerable depths to which the diggings have now penetrated.

Farther in, but still in the lighter areas of the cave, the floor slopes upward toward the dark interior areas and is crowded with burials, of which there are now more than 100 exposed and protected by plexiglass covers for later detailed study. Burials have also been found in the deeper layers of the cave entrances, with the bodies usually contorted, crouched or the head buried alone. The deepest of these discovered so far is the young *Homo sapiens* skull already mentioned as dating back to some 40,000 years ago; and there are other indications as well supporting the conclusion that human culture existed at the time in west Borneo.

PLANTS IN MEDICINE

DICHROA

Wild plants used by local tribes as medicines are often regarded suspiciously by Western doctors. However, the medical value of the four plants shown on these two pages, long known to Asians, is now appreciated by modern medical science. For centuries in China the roots and leaves of Dichroa febrifuga (above) were administered to counter malarial fever. But it was not until 1942 that scientists discovered that a crystalline extract of this herb was as effective as the traditional quinine. The uses of Momordica (below) are varied enough to seem almost magical: the crushed leaves are applied to skin diseases and aching stomachs and heads, while the juice is a purge used to expel parasitic worms. Also, the fruit contains an abortion-producing drug.

MOMORDICA

The Niah *sapiens* skull was found at the 100-inch level in the west mouth excavations in a pit aptly called "hell" because of the extreme heat and discomfort of working there. At this level the deposit is extremely fine and difficult to work; nothing is fossilized and pieces fragment easily. With great patience and skill, trained workers use soft brushes to uncover the relics. Not far below the 100-inch level, bones, both human and animal, and shells have disintegrated completely through the mere process of time. Slowly dehydrated under the peculiar conditions of the great limestone cave, they simply and gradually melted into the dust of ages.

Can further finds be expected under these conditions still deeper down? It is possible. Indications of human activity can be traced, for one thing, by chemical analyses of the "soil," by certain pollens and by the presence of stone tools and fire strikers. It is even possible that at still lower levels at Niah a stage of true fossilization, or in this case limification, may be found. For common sense suggests that even earlier hominids may have been present in Borneo, which was linked by land with the area inhabited by Java man in the Pleistocene. And if conditions were not right for fossilization, there is always the chance of discovery of stone tools. These hopes received dramatic confirmation recently from the discovery, in a bauxite mine 300 miles down the coast from Niah, of two large stone tools which are similar to the Java culture, roughly contemporaneous but not associated with *Pithecanthropus erectus*.

THE Hell Pit of Niah has yielded another find of unusual interest—the bones of the long extinct giant pangolin, *Manis palaeojavanica*. Previously described by Eugene Dubois, from the fossil beds of Kedung Brubus in Java, where it was associated with the mandible of *Pithecanthropus*, this huge, scaly anteater has now been identified by the Dutch paleontologist D. A. Hooijer from a series of bones going as deep as the limit of bone survival. It has not been found in the high levels of the cave, indicating that this animal has been extinct for a very long time. Its smaller congener *Manis javanica* still survives throughout most of the tropical Asian region.

What the higher levels have yielded, however, in the form of literally millions of fragments painstakingly collected and preserved, is an imposing and rapidly increasing record of human culture covering the last 50,000 years. Much of this record is in the form of food animals, much of it is represented by tools. Thus in the Upper Paleolithic, some 30,000 years ago, chopping tools make their appearance, along with remains of orangutans, monkeys, a pig, wild ox, rhinoceros, honey bear and tapir. Fish, lizards, turtles, rats, bats and a few large birds, mostly hornbills which could be caught easily when the female was walled up in a tree-crevice nest by her mate, were also clearly part of the fare. There is even evidence that animal fragments were preserved as charms: pigs' teeth, rhinoceros' teeth and in one case a beautifully preserved rhino leg bone used as a skull pillow in a burial were found. The cult of magic or medicinal charms in Southeast Asia must be very old indeed.

The Sarawak Museum today has just one tiger's tooth from the Niah cave deposits. This tooth, the crown of a young canine, is from the Neolithic levels and it raises some interesting questions. There are no remains of the tiger in earlier levels at Niah. The animal is extinct in Borneo today. Does a single tooth in a late level constitute sufficient evidence for its having belonged to the original fauna? No—the tooth could have been imported by man. Remains from deeper levels are needed to substantiate the tiger's case.

Even so, the extent to which a place like the Niah caves became a center of Stone Age civilization has only barely been indicated at this site. As well as working in the west mouth, the museum staff in the last five years has been exploring the whole limestone foundation of the Niah massif and they have found literally scores of other caves of archeological value. One of these, first identified from the air, involved a group of skilled climbers in five days' preparation and ladder building before they could reach it high up in the cliff. It proved to be a cave almost as impressive as the west mouth itself, and a first scratch at the surface produced positive human results. They have so far excavated extensively in five other caves in the formation. The broad results fit with the west mouth picture; but in every case something new and special has appeared as well—including evidence for a small Neolithic "Negritoid" population living alongside larger people but using separate burial caves (there have been no Negritos on the island in historic times).

Most exciting of all is a beautiful cave high up in a difficult cliff site, its mouth covered with orange, green and purple lichens and mosses. Inside the quiet, cool cavern is what appears at first to be a row of boats "beached" on the dusty floor, their prows pointing inward and carved with fierce crocodile and other animal heads. These are actually "ships of the dead," each one of which originally contained a body and was covered with another dugout-shaped lid. This coffin was then placed upon wooden posts, but all, with the exception of one, have long since fallen over. The floor is littered with human bones and relics of late Stone and early Iron Age rituals for burial, including quantities of early Chinese pottery and other mainland imports, bringing the picture there up into the full Iron Age around the Eighth or Ninth Century A.D.

Some 50 feet farther inside the cave, the sloping ceiling is covered with primitive paintings in the vivid red of hematite iron ore. Crescent-shaped funerary boats, "dancing" figures, the head of a hornbill, fighting cocks and other designs, from a few inches to four feet in size, were applied with heavy strokes of primitive brushes possibly made of the frayed ends of bamboo or bunches of reeds. The artists worked from uncomfortable positions on a narrow ledge running along under the ceiling, choosing this area for their murals because it was the only expanse of white limestone surface available to them that was free of plant growth or animal remains.

THIS "Painted Cave" showed no signs of having been visited by man during several centuries. It is too high and light to contain either of Niah's modern incentives for search—bat guano or edible nests. After reconstructing a picture of what they thought was going on there a thousand or more years ago, the museum experts found that some of the same ideas were present in the folklore and customs of local tribesmen named Punans, some of whom helped in the excavations. They became so interested in this that, with the help of a few of the oldest men, they have been able to revive the old Punan death rites to assist the spirits in the journey of the dead. These death rites clearly go right back into the ancient past.

On the whole, the striking impression gained from all this Niah work is of an advanced culture that was achieved as the Stone Age proceeded in west Borneo. By the later Neolithic, say at 3000 B.C., there were beautifully made, finely polished stone tools—round axes and adzes made of various kinds of stone, shaped and tapered on one side, and quadrangular smaller adzes and chisels of black stone. There was superb pottery decorated in three colors, of

HYDNOCARPUS

Chaulmoogra oil, pressed from the seeds of a tree, Hydnocarpus (above), is one of the most effective medicines in the treatment of leprosy, now called Hansen's disease. The treatment is long and injections of the oil are painful, but it remains a source of hope for many victims, of whom there are some 5,000 in the U.S. alone. Chaulmoogra was praised in ancient Oriental writings but was not used by modern science until 1853. Similarly, a potion made from the root of Rauwolfia serpentina (below) has been employed by Indians for thousands of years in the treatment of insanity. But only in 1952 did Western scientists begin to realize its value; acting on the brain, Rauwolfia tranquilizes psychotic patients, calming even the most violent.

RAUWOLFIA

which over 800 whole or reconstructed pieces have now been collected, and more than 20,000 classified shards. The uniquely patterned pots and dishes, no two alike, have various bands and designs made of red hematite, black soot and yellow clay. This three-color ware, and possibly other pottery, was made at the cave site. There was also an elaboration of shell, bone and stone jewelry, including jade, various fabrics and mats, nets and boats. Many pieces showed what could fairly be described as a love of the dead, extending not only to exquisitely laid out primary burials but also to secondary burial of bones and to cremation, especially of babies—these long predating the Hindu influence to which this custom had hitherto been attributed in Southeast Asia. There is evidence, too, of a tiny domestic dog with short, small teeth, probably a Neolithic lap dog rather than a hunter. It was apparently widespread in western Borneo, as its bones were found not only at Niah but also 400 miles southwest, beyond Kuching. This dog, featured in folklore, is now extinct. It has been completely swamped by the only too familiar, larger and much less sophisticated pye-dog of Borneo, a mongrel type with a down-curled tail.

All of this appears to indicate a dynamic Neolithic culture with a considerable influence, extending far inland into the central highlands and along the coast even to tiny offshore islands.

B Y this later Neolithic period, the Malay peoples, along with related Mongoloids of southern China, were well established throughout the islands, having moved down in massive waves from the mainland. Their intermingling with the earlier inhabitants resulted in a gradual blending and replacement of the Australoid and Negrito elements with Malay stock. Many of the aboriginal peoples were also pushed farther south and east as the invaders settled into the area. In the same fashion, the movements of Caucasoid peoples through India pushed the earlier populations to the fringes of that region. The Burmese mountains prevented the Caucasoid expansion from moving into the eastern part of the mainland and into the islands to the south, but the Malay peoples had no such mountain barriers before them as they swept down the long peninsula and into the island arc.

Throughout the entire region, remnants of the earliest inhabitants remained relatively untouched in remote jungles and hills, passed over by the main waves of newcomers. Their hunting, Stone Age culture persisted for a long time, and a clue to what their life was like can be found among their few descendants in these places today—the Negritos in the Andaman Islands south of Burma, on the Malay Peninsula and in the Philippines; the Australoid hill tribes in India; the Veddoid type peoples of southern India and Ceylon, long, wavy-haired aboriginals with some indistinct relationship to the early Caucasoids and Australoids.

Agriculture, probably slow in developing, was given a real impetus by the spread of the Malay peoples. They were still hunters of wild game but they also had the domestic buffalo and the chicken and pig, although the latter were apparently used at first more for rituals and ceremonies than for food. They cultivated rice and millet as staple foods, and as a source of a beerlike beverage. Their methods of cultivation were either temporary or permanent. In the hill regions a migratory agriculture predominated, a slash-and-burn technique involving a cutting back of the jungle at the end of the dry season and planting seeds with digging sticks. The first season's crop was usually a good one, but after two or three seasons, the soil was worn out. Thus the tribes had necessarily to live a nomadic life, moving from one area to another, letting their fields lie fallow under the creeping jungle for at least 10 years before they returned to cultivate them again.

Lowland cultivation was more permanent, with the development of irrigated fields. Here were grown such staple foods as the banana, breadfruit, turniplike taro and yam. The paper mulberry tree was used for cloth, made from the inner bark which was soaked and beaten into long strips of thin material. These Neolithic peoples also had beautifully polished stone tools, some of semiprecious stones, which they used to cut and carve wood and to build seafaring canoes and wooden houses set above ground on stilts.

With agriculture came a shift from pure hunting to settled communities, and with that the gradual opening of the forest. Here was the second great influence of man on the animal life of the Oriental region. Tools and early domestication of animals had first affected animal populations, and now agriculture began to change the face of the land. The original forests, the habitat of the majority of terrestrial animals, began a slow, inexorable decline. In something like 200 generations man has passed through the Bronze, Iron and Steel ages, in a crescendo of discovery, invention, growth and dispersal of populations, deforestation, consumption of resources and increasing complexity of organizations and ideas. And along with this crescendo of cultural development, animals as a whole were increasingly exposed to a new selective process. As the face of southern Asia and the adjacent islands changed, the knell of the dominant animals began to be sounded.

The earliest of the Malay invaders could probably be recognized today in some of the tribes found in mountain and island remnants from the India-Burma border to the Lesser Sundas. Generally speaking, these peoples have remained on a more primitive level than the descendants of the later immigrant waves, but by the Neolithic they, too, had reached an artistic and cultural level in their personal decorations and in the way in which they embellished their houses. Horns were used for ornament—antlers as well as hornbill horns. They also used large feathers, as the first cave drawings and later pottery designs show. The argus pheasant with its magnificent four-foot ocellated, or eyed, tail feathers was a perfect object for adornment.

W<small>E</small> know argus pheasants today. They are rare but still found in heavy jungle from southern Burma across to Vietnam and south to Borneo. But the double-banded argus is a species known from only a single feather. This one feather in the British Museum is so distinct in pattern that no one doubts it belongs to an extinct species. Where did it live? We can guess it was in Java, where so many animals have become extinct. How tantalizing to know a superb pheasant from a single feather. But if this is tantalizing, how many species have there been that we have just missed knowing!

The advent of irrigation and of the resulting city-states has meant the gradual conquest of the great lowlands of southern Asia and the islands—the deltas, the river plains, the seacoasts fit for harbors and trade. By the beginning of the Bronze Age, trade must have been well developed between the northern and northeastern parts of the mainland and the southern islands. Indian merchants probably entered the area about the Sixth Century B.C., and the Chinese about 300 B.C., and from then on, the world began to draw on the wealth of the Indies. All this has impelled the immutable changes that have been steadily lessening the primary hold of animals in the Oriental region. Trade began early

A MYTH ON COLORATION

The physical characteristics of many mammals and birds have worked their way into the legends of primitive peoples the world over. In Borneo, the brilliant plumage of the argus pheasant (above) and the dullness of the common coucal, or bubut (below), have been woven into a witty story: The pheasant and the bubut agreed to tattoo each other to disguise themselves from their enemies. The bubut did his work well, adorning the pheasant with delicate markings and pretty colors. But the pheasant was too lazy to trouble with the bubut. Crying that enemies were approaching, he dumped the jar of pigments over the bubut's head. The drab blue body and rust-colored wings, the legend ends, attest to the shabby treatment given the bubut by his ally.

HARVESTING BIRDS' NESTS

Poised on a rickety ladder, a collector scrapes nests of cave swiftlets from the ceiling of a cavern in North Borneo. These nests consist largely of dried saliva and are the main ingredient of birds' nest soup, an Oriental delicacy. They are glued to the cave walls in the hundreds of thousands by the swiftlets, whose salivary glands become greatly enlarged during the breeding season.

in these animals themselves. Along with spices, camphorwood and ebony, tropical fruits and other vegetable products, and gold and tin, the animal artifacts attained high value. Ivory, of course, was one of the most important, along with pearls from southern Asia. In return for pottery and ceramic ware, and iron and glass beads from China, the southern realms were sending rhinoceros horn, brightly colored parrots, feathers of many kinds used in jewelry, especially kingfisher feathers, pangolin scales, deer antlers, hornbill ivory, tortoise shell and birds' nests. Only the inaccessibility of many of these creatures prevented them from being exterminated. The helmeted hornbill provided one of the most unusual and valuable sources of trade. Hornbill "ivory" was once more valuable than jade, and when exported to China was very finely carved there into pure ornaments, as belt buckles for mandarins, plume holders, even snuff bottles. According to the Ming dynasty records of tribute from foreign potentates, a piece of hornbill ivory was worth twice the value of a pound of elephant ivory. Fortunately, the Chinese craft, delicate and complicated, of carving these grotesque relics seems to have died out, otherwise we would be curious to know today what the helmeted hornbill must have looked like. It could easily have become another dodo. Some tribes in Borneo still carve the casque, making ornaments for ears, belts and ceremonial swords, but their craft, not as fine as that of the Chinese, is dying out.

PERHAPS the most famous export from the region was—and still is—birds' nests. Birds' nests are harvested all over Southeast Asia, but probably the richest source is in Borneo. Literally millions of small swifts, related to the American chimney swift, nest in limestone caves or rock crevices all over this tropical region, and at least three species make nests against the rocky walls using a protein, related to mucin, which is secreted from the birds' own salivary glands. In contact with air, this material hardens into a rather friable cement. Sometimes mixed with moss or feathers, sometimes in the form of pure spittle, the nest clings precariously to the inner cliff face and is generally harvested before egg laying has commenced. Special nest collectors, their jobs usually hereditary, risk their lives climbing rickety ladders often over 100 feet tall or working from scaffolding held up by rattan ropes, scraping the nests off the walls. Gathered up by assistants off the thick guano floor, the nests are later sorted by type, partially cleaned and then packed in thin little pancakes, easy to ship. Top prices for "white," or clean, nests, those made entirely from spittle, can be as much as $132 a pound and are worth every penny of it. Later on in a Chinese restaurant, prepared lovingly as birds' nest soup with chicken, with pigeon eggs or with crab, they are delectable. Curiously enough, there is little evidence that the trade has been harmful to the swifts. Their second or third nests survive and the next generation carries on.

Would that the other animals could do as well. Our generation has seen an argus pheasant disappear and the pink-headed duck of India lapse into the shadows. Two species of rhinoceros seem headed that way, along with the orangutan, the giant panda, the marsh-loving Eld's deer, the great oxen, the Komodo lizard and perhaps the tiger. As man's numbers increase, as each generation becomes more demanding, our environment and our animal heritage will give way. In the process man finds himself creating inexorable changes. Himself an agent of natural processes, he has the power to affect irrevocably the nature of his world. We owe it to ourselves not to misuse this power and thereby diminish irreversibly our resources and the future of our planet.

IN CROWDED INDIA, MEN AND ANIMALS LIVE IN CLOSE HARMONY. HERE A SACRED COW AND A PEACOCK AMBLE THROUGH A VILLAGE

The Human Landscape

Wild though large sections of the region still are, tropical Asia is also one of the world's most densely populated areas. Wherever its mixture of races and culturally different peoples concentrates, the landscape has been made over in man's image—and terraces and paddy fields, plantations and farms yield exotic crops from native plants, as well as species introduced long ago by Europeans.

A PADAUNG WOMAN, her neck encircled by 50 pounds of brass rings, is representative of the Malay stock predominant in Burma, but her features also indicate Mongoloid blood.

A Medley of People

Who are the people of tropical Asia and how did they come to live where they do? Difficult questions, since the movements of men in this area have never been—and may never be—fully worked out. About all that can be said with any certainty is that the Caucasoids of the Indian peninsula and the Malays to the southeast constitute dominant races. The Australoids and Negritos (right) found in fringe areas are assumed to represent earlier inhabitants, driven there by northern invaders, probably Malays and Mongoloids. And just as the Malays came down into the islands, so too in later years came Indians and Chinese, who, along with Arabs and finally Europeans, have all left their mark upon the area.

A HINDU feeding sacred monkeys at a Benares temple has the Caucasoid face and brown skin characteristic of the majority of people dwelling in India and Pakistan.

A PHILIPPINE NEGRITO in scanty dress typifies the primitive ways of his people—last of a race thought to have been among the first to live in tropical Asia.

MENDING HIS NET, an Iban fisherman shows marks of his tribe
—tattoos and long hair. One of Borneo's Dayak tribes, descendants of the Malay race, the Ibans were formerly head-hunters.

DANCING GRACEFULLY, a Balinese girl reflects the artistic
temperament of her people. Of Malay stock, the Balinese show
the cultural influence of Indian missionaries and merchants.

The Cornucopia
of Tropical Asia

For the people of the region, the year-round warmth and heavy rains of Southeast Asia are a boon, making possible the intensive cultivation of a great variety of economically valuable and nutritious plants. Among the indigenous species raised are many that now have a worldwide distribution. The world would be a poorer place without the cinnamon, cloves, pepper and nutmeg, coconut, soybeans and rice, the lemons, limes, mangoes, oranges and bananas that tropical Asia has bestowed upon it. A demand for commodities like these helped to make the area a focus of trade even in ancient times. As early as 200 B.C., spices from the Moluccas flowed westward through China and Arabia to Egypt and Rome. And long before Europeans dared sail across the uncharted seas, sugar and silks, camphor and sandalwood, pepper and ginger found their way into the markets of the Middle East and the Mediterranean world. When Europeans settled in the area, lured by its potential as well as its riches, they introduced new species from other tropical regions. Today, it is hard to believe that many of the most familiar of these plants, like cassava, rubber and sweet potatoes, were not always a part of the land.

A Leaf to Drink

Tea is to the tropical regions of Asia what wine is to France. It grows on hillsides like this one in Java, often in soil too poor for other crops. Introduced from China and Assam, it flourished throughout the area wherever good drainage carried

off excess water and the climate permitted the plant to recover rapidly after its leaves were removed. Today, India and Ceylon account for almost 75 per cent of the world's export crop. Kept to shrub-size, the tea tree begins to produce when about four years old, and frequent pruning from then on encourages the growth of new shoots. Quality depends to some extent on the age of the leaves picked—the younger the better. Flavor can vary from hillside to hillside, and even from sunlight to shade.

A Versatile Starch

Cassava, one of Indonesia's most important staples, here shows up as a delicacy in shrimp chips, or krupuks, made with its flour. Brought to Asia from tropical America by Europeans in the 18th Century, the cassava plant yields several kinds of starch obtained from its roots and tubers. When soaked, dried, sifted and heated, the starch collects into little lumps—tapioca.

A Protein Treasure

Basketlike fishing boats on the Mettur Dam in south India show the primitive nature of much of the equipment still used today to take fish from the relatively unexploited waters of tropical Asia. Smoked or salted, dried or fried, mixed with chili preserve and eaten with bowls of rice, fish is the sole source of animal protein for millions in this meat-starved area.

Packed with Fire

Thousands of chili peppers drying in an Indian field attest to the popularity of this fiery condiment throughout most of Southeast Asia. Although not indigenous, chili pepper became an ingredient of curries and other dishes in Indonesia and India soon after its introduction by the Portuguese in the early 1600s. The Spaniards, who had picked it up in the West Indies, gave the plant its name to distinguish it from the true pepper of the East Indies, the world's most sought-after spice.

The Flavor of History

Known to the Greeks and Romans, pepper extends even further back into time in its native East Indies, where it has been in use since at least 3000 B.C. As shown here in Malaysia, pepper grows on a vine, from which its seeds are picked before they have fully ripened. During the Middle Ages, it fetched such high prices that European merchants, seeking to do away with the Arab middleman, pushed for a sea route to the Orient—and thereby helped to launch the age of exploration.

A Tree of Many Gifts

The coconut palm is a versatile tree indeed: its trunk provides wood, its roots yield a drug, its fronds are used as thatch, while its nuts furnish meat, milk and even more. Coconut shells can serve as containers or be converted into fine charcoal. The meat, dried into copra, produces an oil from which margarine, soap, shampoo, shaving cream and other goods are made. Because of their economic importance, coconut products constitute chief exports of Ceylon, Indonesia and the Philippines. Cracked by hand (*left*) and set out to dry, from 3,500 to 7,000 coconuts will provide 1,200 pounds of oil plus a valuable end product—800 pounds of oil cake to feed cattle.

A Plant of Many Strands

Despite its name, Manila hemp is not hemp at all, but the water-resistant strands of a wild plantain, related to the banana and developed mainly in the Philippines. Made from leafstalks whose fibers may be 12 feet long, it is processed into marine rope, heavy twine, sacks, wrapping paper and paper bags—and in Japan is used to make movable wall partitions. True hemp, cultivated in other parts of tropical Asia, has similar uses but is grown for other reasons as well. From its seeds comes an oil employed in the manufacture of soap and paint, and from the flowering tops and leaves, a sticky resin, which in its strongest form is hashish and, in wild plants, marijuana.

This Grass Called Rice

Probably of swampy origin, the native grass called rice grows best in flood plains and river valleys. The young shoots, transplanted from seedbeds to flooded fields *(left)*, must stand in four to eight inches of water to attain maximum growth. So valuable is the crop in this area where rice is the main and sometimes only food of millions that human scarecrows may occasionally be employed to guard the fields. But the nutritive value of many species is low and supply invariably fails to meet demand. To rectify this, the International Rice Research Institute in the Philippines is trying to develop a richer and more productive rice than is grown now in Southeast Asia, yet one which satisfies the taste requirements of the people.

LIKE A CRAZED MIRROR, RICE TERRACES REFLECT THE SUN. DEPENDENT UPON SEASONAL RAINS, THEY YIELD BUT ONE CROP A YEAR ▶

Bibliography

Geographic and Regional Descriptions

Banks, E., *A Naturalist in Sarawak.* Kuching Press, 1949.

Cole, Fay Cooper, *The Peoples of Malaysia.* Van Nostrand, 1945.

Cressey, George B., *Asia's Lands and Peoples* (3rd ed.). McGraw-Hill, 1963.

Dobby, E. H. G., *Monsoon Asia.* Quadrangle Books, 1961. *Southeast Asia.* John Wiley, 1951.

Forbes, Henry O., *A Naturalist's Wanderings in the Eastern Archipelago.* Harper, 1885.

Harrison, Brian, *South-East Asia; A Short History.* Macmillan, 1954.

Harrisson, T. H., ed., *Borneo Jungle.* Lindsay Drummond, 1938.

MacDonald, Malcolm, *Angkor.* Frederick A. Praeger, 1959.

Ooi, Jin-bee, *Land, People and Economy in Malaya.* Longmans, Green, 1963.

Shelford, Robert W. C., *A Naturalist in Borneo.* E. P. Dutton, 1917.

Spencer, J. E., *Asia, East by South.* John Wiley, 1954.

Stamp, L. Dudley, *Asia, a Regional and Economic Geography.* E. P. Dutton, 1962.

*Sykes, Sir Percy, *A History of Exploration.* Harper, 1961.

Thomas, P., *Epics, Myths and Legends of India.* D. B. Taraporevala Sons, Bombay, 1955.

Vlekke, Bernard H. M., *Nusantara, A History of Indonesia.* Quadrangle Books, 1960.

*Wallace, Alfred Russel, *The Malay Archipelago.* Dover, 1962.

Wells, Carveth, *Six Years in the Malay Jungle.* Doubleday, 1925.

Winstedt, R. O., ed., *Malaya, the Straits Settlements and the Federated and Unfederated Malay States.* Constable, 1923.

General Wildlife

Burden, W. Douglas, *Look to the Wilderness.* Little, Brown, 1960.

Gee, E. P., *The Wild Life of India.* Collins, 1964.

Mayr, Ernst, *Animal Species and Evolution.* Harvard University Press, 1963.

Pope, Clifford H., *The Giant Snakes.* Alfred A. Knopf, 1961.

†Talbot, Lee Merriam, *A Look at Threatened Species.* I.U.C.N., 1960.

Tweedie, M. W. F., and J. L. Harrison, *Malayan Animal Life.* Longmans, Green, 1955. *The*

Snakes of Malaya (2nd ed.). Government Printing Office, Singapore, 1961.

Plants

Corner, Edred J. H., *Wayside Trees of Malaya* (2 parts, 2nd ed.). Government Printing Office, Singapore, 1952.

Hill, Albert F., *Economic Botany.* McGraw-Hill, 1952.

Holttum, R. E., *Plant Life in Malaya.* Longmans, Green, 1954.

Jones, Lester W., ed., *A Treasury of Spices.* American Spice Trade Association, 1956.

Kreig, Margaret B., *Green Medicine.* Rand McNally, 1964.

Merrill, Elmer D., *Plant Life of the Pacific World.* Macmillan, 1945.

Richards, P. W., *Tropical Rain Forest.* Cambridge University Press, 1957.

Ridley, H. N., *Flora of the Malay Peninsula* (5 parts). L. Reeve, 1922-1925.

Schimper, A. F. W., *Plant Geography upon a Physiological Basis.* Hafner, 1960.

Wickizer, V. D., and M. K. Bennett, *The Rice Economy of Monsoon Asia.* Food Research Institute, Stanford, California, 1941.

Mammals

Alpers, Antony, *Dolphins; The Myth and the Mammal.* Houghton Mifflin, 1961.

Boulenger, E. G., *Apes and Monkeys.* Robert M. McBride, 1888.

Carrington, Richard, *Elephants: A Short Account of Their Natural History, Evolution and Influence on Mankind.* Basic Books, 1959.

Carter, T. D., J. E. Hill, and G. H. H. Tate, *Mammals of the Pacific World.* Macmillan, 1945.

Davis, D. Dwight, *Mammals of the Lowland Rain Forest of North Borneo.* Bulletin of National Museum, No. 31, Singapore, September, 1962.

†Harper, Francis, *Extinct and Vanishing Mammals of the Old World.* American Committee for International Wildlife Protection, 1945.

Harrisson, Barbara, *Orang-utan.* Doubleday, 1963.

Hooton, E. A., *Up from the Ape* (rev. ed.). Macmillan, 1947.

Tate, G.H.H., *Mammals of Eastern Asia.* Macmillan, 1947.

Yerkes, Robert M., and Ada Yerkes, *The Great Apes.* Yale University Press, 1929.

Birds

Ali, Sálim, *Indian Hill Birds.* Oxford University Press, 1949. *The Birds of Sikkim.* Oxford University Press, 1962. *The Birds of Travancore and Cochin.* Oxford University Press, 1953.

Bates, R.S.P., and E.H.N. Lowther, *Breeding Birds of Kashmir.* Oxford University Press, 1952.

Beebe, William, *Pheasants, Their Lives and Homes.* Doubleday, 1926.

Delacour, Jean T., *Birds of Malaysia.* Macmillan, 1947. *The Pheasants of the World.* Charles Scribner, 1951.

Delacour, Jean T., and Ernst Mayr, *Birds of the Philippines.* Macmillan, 1946.

Glenister, A. G., *The Birds of the Malay Peninsula, Singapore and Penang.* Oxford University Press, 1951.

Henry, G. M., *A Guide to the Birds of Ceylon.* Oxford University Press, 1955.

MacDonald, Malcolm, *Birds in My Indian Garden.* Alfred A. Knopf, 1961.

Madoc, G. C., *An Introduction to Malayan Birds.* The Malayan Nature Society, 1956.

Ripley, S. Dillon, *A Synopsis of the Birds of India and Pakistan.* Bombay Natural History Society, 1961. *Consideration of the Origin of the Indian Avifauna.* National Institute of Sciences of India, Proceedings, 1953. *The Bird Fauna of the West Sumatra Islands.* Bulletin of the Museum of Comparative Zoology, Harvard University, 1944.

Smythies, Bertram E., *Birds of Borneo.* Oliver and Boyd, 1960. *The Birds of Burma.* Oliver and Boyd, 1940.

Tweedie, M.W.F., *Common Malayan Birds.* Longmans, Green, 1960.

Whistler, F.Z.S. Hugh, *Popular Handbook of Indian Birds.* Gurney and Jackson, 1941.

Insects

Corbet, A. Steven, and H. M. Pendlebury, *Butterflies of the Malay Peninsula* (2nd rev. ed.). Oliver and Boyd, 1956.

Curran, C. H., *Insects of the Pacific World.* Macmillan, 1946.

Klots, Alexander B., and Elsie B. Klots, *Living Insects of the World.* Doubleday, 1959.

Reitter, Ewald, *Beetles.* G. P. Putnam, 1961.

Wheeler, William Morton, *Social Life Among the Insects.* Harcourt Brace, 1923.

Geology

Bemmelen, R. W. van, *The Geology of Indonesia* (Vol. IA). Nijhoff, 1949.

Bullard, Fred M., *Volcanoes in History, in Theory, in Eruption.* University of Texas, 1962.

Matthew, William D., *Climate and Evolution.* New York Academy of Sciences, 1939.

Umbgrove, J.H.F., *Structural History of the East Indies.* Cambridge University Press, 1949.

Wadia, D. N., *Geology of India* (3rd ed.). Macmillan, 1953.

Zeuner, Friederich E., *Dating the Past* (4th rev. ed.). Longmans, Green, 1958.

Miscellaneous

Aubert de la Rüe, Edgar, François Bourlière, and Jean-Paul Harroy, *The Tropics.* Alfred A. Knopf, 1957.

Beaufort, L. F. de, *Zoogeography of the Land and Inland Waters.* Macmillan, 1951.

Coon, Carleton S., *The Origin of Races.* Alfred A. Knopf, 1962. *The Story of Man.* Alfred A. Knopf, 1962.

Kendrew, W. G., *The Climates of the Continents* (5th ed.). Clarendon Press, 1961.

Linton, Ralph, *The Tree of Culture.* Alfred A. Knopf, 1955.

Nairn, A.E.M., *Descriptive Palaeoclimatology.* Interscience Publishers, 1961.

Riehl, Herbert, *Tropical Meteorology.* McGraw-Hill, 1954.

Rowland, Benjamin, *The Art and Architecture of India.* Penguin Books, 1953.

Trewartha, Glenn T., *An Introduction to Climate.* McGraw-Hill, 1954.

Williams, Edward Thomas, *A Short History of China.* Harper, 1928.

World Weather Records 1941-50. U.S. Govt. Printing Office, 1959.

Zeuner, Friederich E., *A History of Domesticated Animals.* Hutchinson, 1963.

*Zimmer, Heinrich, *Myths and Symbols in Indian Art and Civilization.* Pantheon, 1946.

*Also available in paperback edition.

†Only available in paperback edition.

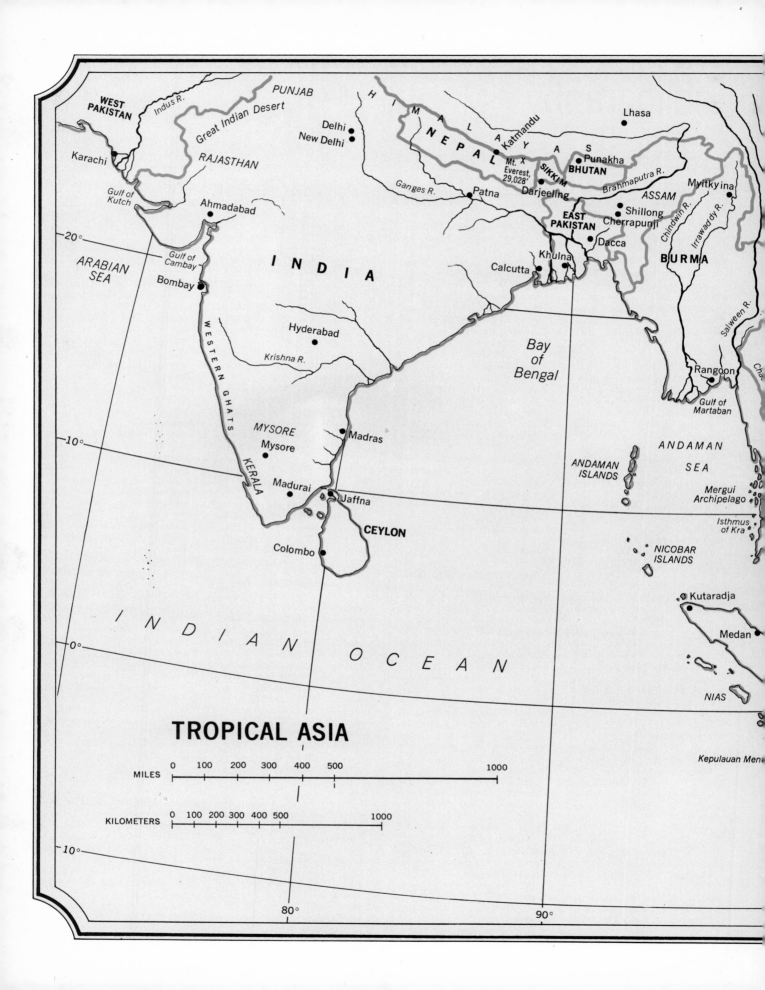

WEST PAKISTAN

Indus R.

PUNJAB

Great Indian Desert

H I M A L A Y A S

Lhasa

Delhi
New Delhi

Katmandu

N E P A L

Mt. X
Everest,
29,028'

SIKKIM

Punakha

BHUTAN

RAJASTHAN

Karachi

*Gulf of
Kutch*

Ganges R.

Patna

Darjeeling

Brahmaputra R.

ASSAM

Myitkyina

Chindwin R.

Irrawaddy R.

Ahmadabad

**EAST
PAKISTAN**

Shillong
Cherrapunji

*Gulf of
Cambay*

Dacca

BURMA

Khulna

20°

**ARABIAN
SEA**

Bombay

Calcutta

I N D I A

Hyderabad

Krishna R.

*Bay
of
Bengal*

W E S T E R N   G H A T S

Salween R.

10°

Rangoon

MYSORE

Mysore

Madras

*Gulf of
Martaban*

ANDAMAN

ANDAMAN
ISLANDS

SEA

K E R A L A

Madurai

Jaffna

*Mergui
Archipelago*

Colombo

CEYLON

*Isthmus
of Kra*

NICOBAR
ISLANDS

Kutaradja

Medan

0°

I N D I A N   O C E A N

NIAS

TROPICAL ASIA

Kepulauan Men─

| MILES | 0 | 100 | 200 | 300 | 400 | 500 | | 1000 |

| KILOMETERS | 0 | 100 200 300 400 500 | | 1000 |

10°

80°

90°

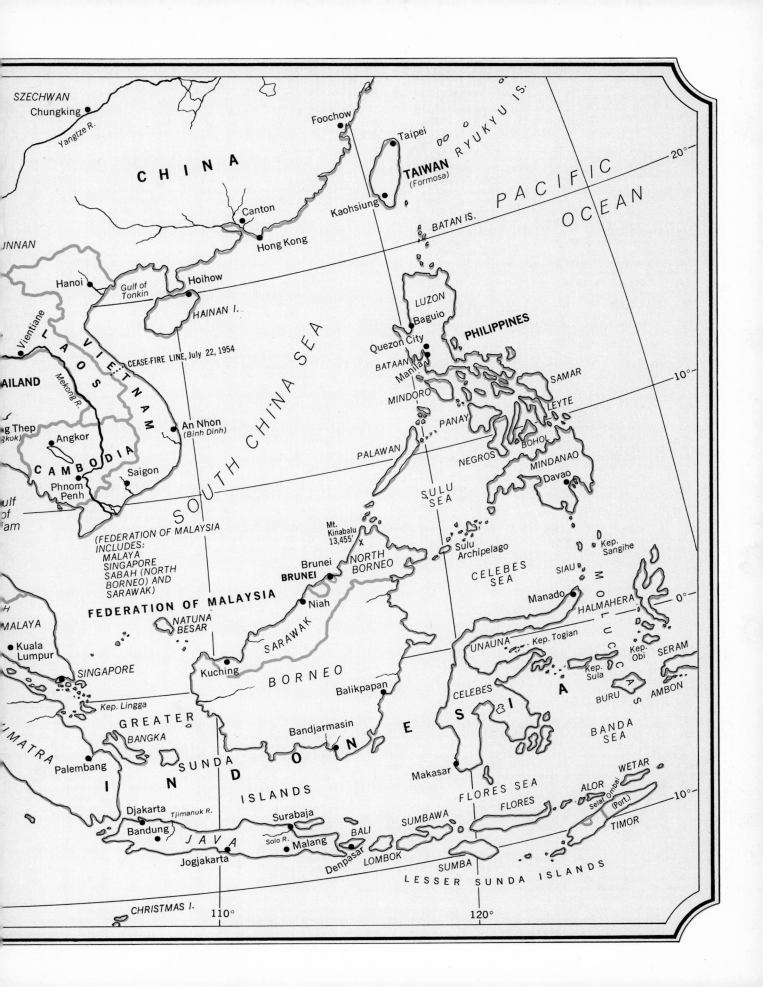

Credits

The sources for the illustrations in this book are shown below.
Credits for pictures from left to right are separated by commas, top to bottom by dashes.

Cover—Marilyn Silverstone from Nancy Palmer Photo Agency
8, 9—John Launois from Black Star
10, 11—maps by Gaetano Di Palma
14—drawings by Lowell Hess
17—Van Bucher from Photo Researchers Inc.
18, 19—map by Matt Greene
20, 21—Dmitri Kessel
22, 23—Stephanie Dinkins from Photo Researchers Inc.
24—Jane Burton from Photo Researchers Inc.
25—Eliot Elisofon
26, 27—Robert E. Huke
28, 29—Michael Rougier
30—Brian Brake from Magnum courtesy of Kumar Sangram Singh
33—drawing by Guy Coheleach
34—drawing by Gaetano Di Palma
39—Stephanie Dinkins
40, 41—Alfred B. Graf, Joseph Nettis
42, 43—Frank Schreider
44—John Dominis
45—James Burke
46, 47—James Burke except bottom right Brian Brake from Magnum
50—T. S. Lal from PIP Photos
53—drawings by Barbara Wolff
55—drawings by Gaetano Di Palma
56, 57—drawings by Matt Greene
58—drawings by John Yrizarry
61—F.G.H. Allen

62, 63—drawing by Lowell Hess
64—Clive R. Jones
65—B. E. Smythies, D. Dwight Davis—N. S. Haile
66—Lim Boo Liat
67—D. Dwight Davis
68, 69—John R. Hendrickson, Beamish Productions Ltd.—Ivan Polunin
70, 71—Geoffrey and Betty Allen, Christina Loke
72—Nina Leen—Tom Harrisson; carving property of Tom Harrisson
73—K. F. Wong
74—Sven Gillsater
75—T. S. Lal from PIP Photos
76, 77—O. C. Edwards
78—Freelance Photographers Guild
83—drawings by Enid Kotschnig
85—drawing by Gaetano Di Palma
86, 87—drawings by Enid Kotschnig
89, 90, 91—Michael Rougier
92, 93—Ivan Polunin, Svend E. Sandermann Olsen
94—Jane Burton from Photo Researchers Inc. except top left Michael Rougier, John Dominis
95—Jane Burton from Photo Researchers Inc. except top left John Dominis
96—Ivan Polunin—Michael Rougier
97—Jane Burton from Photo Researchers Inc.
98, 99—Pierre Pfeffer courtesy

Museum d'Histoire Naturelle, Paris, Ivan Polunin
100—Carl Withner
102—map by Gaetano Di Palma
104—drawing by Otto van Eersel
106, 107—drawings by Joseph Cellini
109 through 112—Michael Rougier
113—Robert Morton
114, 115—Michael Rougier
116—F.G.H. Allen, Christina Loke
117—Hedda Morrison
118, 119—Sven Gillsater
120—Michael Tweedie
122, 123—drawings by Enid Kotschnig
124, 125—drawings by Lowell Hess
126—drawings by Enid Kotschnig
129—E. Hanumantha Rao
130, 131—F.G.H. Allen except top left E. S. Ross
132, 133—Michael Rougier, Jane Burton from Photo Researchers Inc.
134, 135—John R. Hendrickson
136, 137—H. T. Pagden
138—Sven Gillsater
139—D. Dwight Davis
140, 141—Lee Boltin
142—Globe Photos
144—drawing by Rudolf Freund
147—drawing by Enid Kotschnig
148—drawings by Otto van Eersel
150—drawing by Lowell Hess
153—E. Hanumantha Rao
154, 155—Peter Throckmorton from Nancy Palmer Photo

Agency
156—E. P. Gee—Ylla from Rapho-Guillumette
157—Ylla from Rapho-Guillumette
158, 159—E. Schumacher
160—Robert Laffont courtesy *L'Homme et L'Animal*
161—right Ylla from Rapho-Guillumette
162, 163—Ylla from Rapho-Guillumette, Hank Walker
164, 165—Ylla from Rapho-Guillumette
169—drawing by Gaetano Di Palma
170, 171—drawings by Barbara Wolff
173—drawings by Rudolf Freund
174—drawing by Anthony Saris
175—Ylla from Rapho-Guillumette
176—Paul Almasy
177—Robert E. Huke, Svend E. Sandermann Olsen
178—E. F. Brunig
179—Louis Faurer
180, 181—Helen and Frank Schreider
182, 183—Howard Sochurek
184—H. D. Shourie
185—courtesy The Royal Tropical Institute, Amsterdam
186, 187—Horace Bristol—Johnny Florea
188, 189—John Dominis, Margaret Bourke-White
190, 191—Horace Bristol
192, 193—map by Bill Dove
Back Cover—Otto van Eersel

Acknowledgments

The editors of this book are particularly indebted to Tom Harrisson, Director, Sarawak Museum, Kuching, Sarawak, Malaysia, and to Robert F. Inger, Curator of Reptiles, Chicago Natural History Museum, who read the text in its entirety. They also want to thank the following associates of the American Museum of Natural History: Sydney Anderson, Associate Curator, Department of Mammalogy; Alice Gray, Scientific Assistant, Department of Entomology; Sidney Horenstein, Scientific Assistant, Department of Fossil Invertebrates; Karl F. Koopman, Assistant Curator, Department of Mammalogy; Charles E. O'Brien, Assistant Curator, Department of Ornithology; Harry L. Shapiro, Chairman, Department of Anthropology; Richard G. Van Gelder, Chairman and Associate Curator, Department of Mammalogy; and the Museum's library staff.

The editors also want to thank James W. Atz, Editor and Research Associate, Bingham Oceanographic Laboratories, Yale University; François Bourlière, Professor, Faculté de Médecine de Paris; Josephine Burke; Carleton S. Coon, Professor of Anthropology, University of Pennsylvania; Lee S. Crandall, General Curator Emeritus, New York Zoological Park; Jocelyn Crane, Director, Department of Tropical Research, New York Zoological Society; Joseph A. Davis, Jr., Curator of

Mammals, New York Zoological Park; Gordon E. Dunn, Chief Tropical Meteorologist, United States Department of Commerce; Ainslie T. Embree, Assistant Professor of Indian History, Columbia University; John S. Garth, Curator of Collections, Allan Hancock Foundation, University of Southern California; Harold J. Grant, Jr., Chairman, Department of Insects, Academy of Natural Sciences of Philadelphia; Barbara Harrisson; Nasly Heeramaneck; D. A. Hooijer, Rijksmuseum van Natuurlijke Historie, Leiden, Netherlands; Richard Howard, Director, Arnold Arboretum, Harvard University; Robert Jones, Senior Librarian, New York Botanical Garden; Richard M. Klein, Curator of Plant Physiology, New York Botanical Garden; Herbert W. Levi, Associate Curator of Arachnology, Museum of Comparative Zoology, Harvard University; Herbert Riehl, Head, Department of Atmospheric Science, Colorado State University; Elwyn L. Simons, Associate Curator, Vertebrate Paleontology, Yale University; Kumar Sangram Singh; Nirmaljt Singh, Information Officer, Indian Permanent Mission to the U.N.; Charles Thor, Associate Professor, Maritime College, State University of New York; M. W. F. Tweedie, former Director, Raffles Museum, Singapore; Carl Withner, Associate Professor of Biology, Brooklyn College; and P. R. Wycherley, Malayan Nature Society.

Index

Production Staff for Time Incorporated
Arthur R. Murphy Jr. (Vice President and Director of Production), Robert E. Foy, James P. Menton, Caroline Ferri and Robert E. Fraser
Text photocomposed under the direction of Albert J. Dunn and Arthur J. Dunn

x

Printed by R. R. Donnelley & Sons Company, Crawfordsville, Indiana,
and by Livermore and Knight Co., a division of Printing Corporation of America, Providence, Rhode Island
Bound by R. R. Donnelley & Sons Company, Crawfordsville, Indiana
Paper by The Mead Corporation, Dayton, Ohio
Cover stock by The Plastic Coating Corporation, Holyoke, Massachusetts